HISTORICAL SNAPSHOTS OF THE GREAT

ABOUT THE AUTHOR

John Mucai holds a Ph.D. in Business Administration from the University of Nairobi. He is a Certified Public Accountant of Kenya too. He is an alumnus of United States International University, where he graduated with an MSc in Management and Organization Development, and cum laude in BSc in Information Systems & Technology. He retired from Coca-Cola East & Central Africa Ltd in 2017 and has since been pursuing various hobbies and entrepreneurial interests.

Other books in the MUCAI Quick Read series include:

HISTORICAL SNAPSHOTS OF THE GREAT

What can we learn from them?

John Mucai

To my wife, Susan, my son Allan, and my daughter Anne, all of whom are the primary source of inspiration and encouragement for the MUCAI Quick Read Series books project.

Be not afraid of greatness. Some are born great, some achieve greatness, and others have greatness thrust upon them.
—WILLIAM SHAKESPEARE

CONTENTS

FOREWORD

"HISTORICAL SNAPSHOTS OF THE GREAT" is the fourth in the MUCAI Quick Read series. The guiding principle of the series is to offer the reader a unique opportunity to quickly read something useful and yearn to enjoy reading more books in the series.

PREFACE

I FIND IT FASCINATING THAT we live a life shaped to a significant extent by the actions of just a few individuals. These individuals emerged in different parts of the world and did things that profoundly changed history. What is even more amazing is that these individuals emerged from multiple spheres of life: religion, philosophy, science, technology, business, and politics, just to mention a few.

The question that must be asked is: Was there something common amongst these individuals, such as a character trait, their education, and the like? An answer to this question could help us nurture the selected attributes that are most meaningful to mankind's sustained progress.

Finding an answer to this question is a challenge. But just as some of the historical greats showed us, using a well-designed system of pulleys and levers, even heavy loads can be lifted easily. The same metaphor is used in the present book by employing intellectual pulleys and levers to lift heavy mental weights.

Enjoy!

ACKNOWLEDGMENTS

The Almighty is the shining guiding light in my life, even in this book project. I will always remain steadfastly thankful to Him.

This book project would not have been possible without the support of my wife, Susan, my son Allan, and my daughter Anne. All of them provided invaluable assistance in reviewing the book. I owe them a significant debt of gratitude.

I would also like to thank Teddy Muhia Mucai and Nzisa Kattambo for their invaluable contributions in reviewing the book.

INTRODUCTION

Indeed, we should use such discovery as an opportunity
to investigate more exactly the properties discovered
and to prove or disprove them; in both cases we may
learn something useful.
—*Leonhard Euler*

WHAT CONSTITUTES GREATNESS? This question can have many answers depending upon the person asking it, the person giving a response, and the question's context. Therefore, it is essential to do some level setting at the outset to ensure that we are fully aligned as we progress on uncovering the commonalities of the people we consider great.

The Oxford Desk Dictionary gives eight definitions of the word great:

1 of size, extent, or intensity considerably above the normal or the average. 2 important; preeminent; grand; imposing 3 remarkable in ability, character, etc. 4 (foll. by at) adroit;

John Mucai

skilled 5 enthusiastic (great believer in tolerance) 6 Colloq. very pleasurable; enjoyable (had a great time) 7 (in comb.) (in family relationships) denoting one degree further removed upward or downward (great-uncle; great-great-grand-child) -n 8 outstanding person or thing.[1]

In the context of this book, greatness refers to an attribute that we ascribe to an individual because of the profound impact that the person has had in promoting the well-being of mankind. And to deepen our understanding of the drivers of greatness, this book looks at two or more individuals in each significant domain of human life. The only exceptions are in the "business" and "economics" domains. In the business domain, the book covers only Henry Ford, the single businessman in the Biography Online list of the world's 100 most influential people[2]. In economics, the book covers John Maynard Keynes because of the enormous impact his ideas had on the economies of many nations in the world.

The review is performed in alphabetical order in terms of the various domains of human endeavor and chronological order in terms of the individuals covered in each area. The exception is in the realm of "religion." In this case, the review of religious figures follows the size of followership. This approach should eliminate any potential perceptions of bias

The decision to include or exclude a particular historical figure is entirely that of the author. The utmost prudence was applied to ensure that the historical figures selected offer a good representation of the most influential individuals in a particular domain.

The domains of human endeavor covered in the book are activism, art, and business; economics, exploration, and literature; monarchy, music, and philosophy; politics, religion, science, and technology; and sports and writing. Individuals may have influenced more than one life domain. However, for this book's purposes, each person is covered under only one area - the one in which the person had the most significant impact relative to the other domains.

Is there something that we can learn and replicate from the historical greats, or were they just unique human beings who were anointed to accomplish a particular purpose? In other words, what was special about them? And can we develop the same kind of specialness, or at least nurture the young generation so that they can grow to become exceptional as well?

PART ONE

The Great Ones

CHAPTER 1

Activism

*I learned that courage was not the absence of fear but
the triumph over it. The brave man is not he who does
not feel afraid, but he who conquers that fear.*
—*Nelson Mandela*

I HAVE MANY VIVID MEMORIES of Naivasha
Boarding School, a school that I joined in 1968 at the age
of nine at Standard Five, and left three years later to join
high school. One afternoon sometime in the third term of 1968
is particularly memorable. My close friend John William
Kibiribiri, popularly known as JK, subdued one *Gakoma*, a
much bigger boy two classes ahead of us, bringing to an end
Gakoma's reign of terror in the school as a "bully per
excellence." JK's heroism reminds me of the quests for
freedom and justice by Malcolm X, Martin Luther King Jr., and
Nelson Mandela. Certain character traits made these four
individuals great.

One sunny Friday afternoon sometime in the third term of 1968, my close friend John William Kibiribiri, popularly known as JK, and I were sitting on a concrete slab near Aggrey House, one of the three school dormitories at Naivasha Boarding School. It was an ominous moment, as we knew that *Gakoma* (not his real name), the worst school bully at the time, would be at it again.

Gakoma had become a total menace. When he was in a bad mood, any boy who crossed his path would pay a heavy price through an assault. And no boy could even dare report him to the school authorities for fear of an even worse attack later on. But on this particular day, JK had resolved that he was not going to put up with *Gakoma's* constant harassment.

And sure enough, *Gakoma* did show up, not unexpectedly, because the school was small, and his presence could be felt everywhere.

When *Gakoma* saw me and JK, he came towards us like a hungry hyena, and without any warning, started interrogating us in his usual brazen and intimidating manner. He was looking for a fight. But JK was well prepared.

After a short verbal altercation, *Gakoma* went after JK. He pulled JK by the shirt and threw a punch at him. JK blocked the blow. JK unleashed an uppercut that completely disoriented *Gakoma*. Within a few seconds, a minor brawl developed into an all-out war. Several other boys gathered around to watch the two fighters, most of them cheering for JK

I could hardly believe my eyes. JK had transformed into a different human being. He threw several Mohamed Ali-type jabs at *Gakoma* in quick succession. *Gakoma* tried to throw similar jabs, but they were too feeble to have any meaningful impact. At some point, both fighters were wrestling on the ground, but *Gakoma* could simply not match the strength and determination of JK

After receiving a few heavy blows from JK while lying belly up with JK firmly sitting on his stomach, *Gakoma* somehow found some wiggle room and stood up. The boys expected the drama to continue for several minutes. However, *Gakoma* could not withstand the pain and humiliation any longer. He ran away like a coward. And from that moment, there was peace at Naivasha Boarding School.

JK became a hero for subduing the worst, probably mentally deranged, bully of the school. Up to this day, I have never quite figured out what may have created such a cruel human being as *Gakoma*.

Gakoma meant "a small devil," a nickname that the bully earned for his endless acts of terror against Standard Five boys, particularly the young ones who could not fight back.

The sad part was that *Gakoma* meted out his violence against other boys for several months, with total impunity. Every child in Standard Five had to conform. It took the courage of just one boy, JK, to change the situation.

When I was a young kid, one of my uncles once told me something interesting about cats. He said that if you locked an innocent cat in a room and started beating it, the cat would turn against you sooner or later and attack you in a manner that you would not have imagined. *Gakoma* certainly learned this lesson the hard and practical way.

The story of JK and *Gakoma* has many similarities with Malcolm X, Martin Luther King Jr, and Nelson Mandela. These three individuals spent many years struggling hard for the liberation of the black community.

Malcolm X

MANY WRITERS AND SCHOLARS HAVE told the story of Malcolm X. A movie was even made that depicts his life, including his rise as one of the most influential civil rights activists in America.

However, for the purposes of this book, I was curious to find out what gave rise to the Malcolm X phenomenon. It did not take long for me to realize that I was looking at a situation similar to that of my primary school hero, JK.

Malcolm Little was born in 1925 in Omaha, Nebraska. He died in March 1964, at the young age of only 40, after assassination by three members of the Nation of Islam.

During his short life, Malcolm X caused significant waves in the civil rights movement in America, which can still be felt up to this day. Indeed, as I write this book in February 2020, the Office of the District Attorney in New York has announced that it will review the 1965 case of the assassination of Malcolm X. This announcement follows unanswered questions that emerged from a Netflix documentary about the results of the investigation by the Federal Bureau of Investigation (FBI) that led to the conviction of three people who allegedly murdered Malcolm X[3].

A review of Malcolm's history reveals several factors that converged to create the Malcolm X phenomenon. Firstly, he grew up in an environment full of racial hatred. His father was a church minister who was the target of white supremacists, who at one time torched Malcolm's family home. Malcolm's father was killed in yet unexplained circumstances. It was reasonable for Malcolm and his siblings to assume that the white supremacists were responsible for this heinous crime. It is therefore not difficult to imagine what these acts of hatred would have done to the young impressionable mind of Malcolm Little.

Malcolm Little had the ambition to become a lawyer. However, when he expressed this desire to one of his eighth-grade teachers, the teacher told him that carpentry would be a more suitable profession. It is not a wonder that he dropped out of school, perhaps out of despair. He ended up in the streets of Boston and New York, working as a drug dealer and a pimp. This life of crime was short-lived. He ended up in jail.

So, hate had bred despair. Despair had bred resentment. The combination of these two had bred a careless life of crime. And crime had led young Malcolm straight to jail.

I am not a psychologist, but I conjecture that the incarceration of Malcolm Little is what created the Malcolm X phenomenon. Notably, the reading that he did when he was in jail. He was like a cat in a small room that had to fight back to survive.

When Malcolm X came out of jail, he had transformed into a courageous young man with a conviction about his civil and human rights. He had become deeply religious and had converted into a follower of the Muslim religion. He had joined the Nation of Islam (NOI), an organization led by his mentor Elijah Mohamed. He had also changed his name from Malcolm Little to Malcolm X[4].

Sometime in 1964, he visited Mecca in Saudi Arabia. Upon returning to the USA from his pilgrimage, he changed his name from Malcolm X to el-Hajj Malik el-Shabazz.

Later on, when Malcolm X discovered Elijah's infidelities, he could not stand it and decided to leave NOI and set up his own organization.

He was steadfast in his conviction about the equality of all human beings. Further, he did not flinch about it, despite the anxiety that he was causing within the political establishment and within the black community.

So, his greatness emerged from his strength of character and his deep conviction in equal rights for all human beings. His charisma, which I believe was a product of his beliefs, was also part of it. He was not ready to stick with the status quo, which had injured his human dignity since early childhood.

He was not ready to conform to the status quo despite the inherent danger. He was not afraid to speak his mind. And he was exceptionally articulate about it, perhaps a tribute to the extensive reading he had done while he was in jail. He once said that:

> My alma mater was books, a good library... I could spend the rest of my life reading, just satisfying my curiosity."
> "I have often reflected upon the new vistas that reading opened to me. I knew right there in prison that reading had changed the course of my life forever. As I see it today, the ability to read awoke in me some long dormant craving to be mentally alive.[5]

Many of the things that Malcolm X said resonated with millions of people. These people felt that the government had deprived them of their civil liberties, but they did not have the courage or the space to speak up and be heard. Malcolm effectively became their *de facto* leader.

Martin Luther King, Jr.

MARTIN LUTHER KING JR. WAS born in 1929, four years after Malcolm X. He was born in Atlanta, Georgia. He also died young in 1968 at the age of only 39, also through the bullet of an assassin.

Martin Luther King Jr. was born into a religious family. His father was a pastor, and his mother, an active member of the church. These facts are remarkably similar to those of Malcolm X. Still, the reasons for his greatness are in sharp contrast to those related to Malcolm X. However, both individuals were trying to achieve the same goal.

Martin Luther King Jr. loved education. He studied to the highest level possible, achieving a Ph.D. in systematic theology at Boston University.

Martin Luther King is probably the most famous black American civil rights activist in living memory. He had a deep conviction in achieving his vision of liberation for the black people through non-violence.

The vision and legacy of Martin Luther King Jr. are encapsulated in his famous "I have a dream" speech on August

28, 1963. The speech contained slightly more than 30 paragraphs, each of which was loaded with immense passion and emotion. It was an immensely powerful speech that has been cited numerous times in literature relating to liberation struggles[6]. Below is an excerpt.

> *I have a dream that one day this nation will rise up and live out the true meaning of its creed: "We hold these truths to be self-evident: that all men are created equal." I have a dream that one day on the red hills of Georgia, the sons of former slaves and the sons of former slave owners will be able to sit down together at a table of brotherhood.[7]*

But what triggered the Martin Luther King Jr. phenomenon that transformed him into a historical figure?

America was a deeply segregated society with various injustices experienced by black Americans daily. Martin Luther King Jr. must have lived and conformed to the injustices like many other black Americans.

However, like a cat cornered in a room by its master, the arrest of the civil rights activist, Rosa Park, in Montgomery Alabama, for refusing to give up her seat in a bus to a white person (an incident that provoked outrage across America) incensed Martin Luther King Jr intensely. On December 5th, 1955, he organized a boycott of the Montgomery buses by the black community. The boycott lasted 381 days. My view is that that single incident created the Martin Luther King Jr. phenomenon. He was unstoppable after that[8].

John Mucai

He drew inspiration from his Christian beliefs and chose to pursue activism through non-violence.

His non-violence cause was so effective that it earned him the Nobel Peace Prize in 1964. He donated the monetary award to the civil rights movement.

In the Nobel Peace Prize Committee speech on December 10, 1964, Jahn Gunnar Jahn, Chairman of the Nobel Committee, started by making direct reference to the Montgomery bus boycott. He described how Martin Luther King Jr. had charted a course of nonviolent resistance that had inspired the black community in America and other people in the world to consider resolving disputes through peaceful means[9].

One of the things that struck me intensely in Gunnar Jahn's speech was his description of Martin Luther's views on knowledge[10]:

Martin Luther King's belief is rooted first and foremost in the teaching of Christ, but no one can really understand him unless aware that he has been influenced also by the great thinkers of the past and the present. He has been inspired above all by Mahatma Gandhi, whose example convinced him that it is possible to achieve victory in an unarmed struggle. Before he had read about Gandhi, he had almost concluded that the teaching of Jesus could only be put into practice as between individuals; but after making a study of Gandhi he realized that he had been mistaken.

"Gandhi" he says, "was probably the first person in history to lift the love ethic of Jesus above mere interaction between individuals to a powerful and effective social force …"

In Gandhi's teaching he found the answer to a question that had long troubled him: How does one set about carrying out a social reform?

"I found" he tells us, "in the nonviolent resistance philosophy of Gandhi … the only morally and practically sound method open to oppressed people in their struggle for freedom."

Martin Luther's pursuit of this course was relentless, sometimes leading to his imprisonment, threats to his life, and ultimately his death on April 4, 1968.

It is quite surprising that a person seeking justice through nonviolent means would become such a big threat to some people. They felt that he was such a big that they had to permanently eliminate him from the face of the earth.

Once again, we see a hero whose heroism is rooted in an immense desire for justice. This desire has a foundation in knowledge of struggles that he acquired from past and contemporary thinkers.

Nelson Mandela

NELSON MANDELA (1918 – 2013) WAS a South African political activist who spent the better part of his youth and adult life in prison. However, unlike Malcolm X and Martin Luther King Jr., Mandela lived to the ripe old age of 95. He passed away at his home in Houghton, Johannesburg, South Africa, in the presence of his family.

John Mucai

Nelson Mandela received a Nobel Peace Prize in 1993 (jointly with F.W. de Klerk) for his exceptionally unwavering efforts in seeking a solution to racial segregation in South Africa.

Similar to Malcolm X and Martin Luther King Jr., Nelson Mandela loved education. He studied at the University College of Fort Hare and the University of Witwatersrand, where he earned a law degree in 1942.

Like Malcolm X and Martin Luther King Jr., he was also much incensed by racial segregation under the apartheid system. However, unlike Malcolm X and Martin Luther King Jr., he decided to pursue armed struggle.

He committed his life to fighting racial inequality and injustice under the apartheid system, eventually landing in jail after missing the death sentence literally by a whisker.

During the trial in April 1964, which was followed closely by many people worldwide, he made two statements that epitomized his philosophy and vision:

We believe that South Africa belongs to all the people who live in it and not to one group, be it black or white. We did not want an interracial war and tried to avoid it to the last minute.

During my lifetime, I have dedicated myself to this struggle of the African people. I have fought against white domination, and I have fought against black domination. I have cherished the ideal of a democratic and free society in which all persons live together in harmony and with equal opportunities. It is an ideal which I hope to live for and to achieve. But if needs be, it is an ideal for which I am prepared to die.

The fact that Mandela would spend 27 years seeking justice and equality for his fellow citizens is one of the amazing realities of history.

CHAPTER 2

Art

Learn the rules like a pro, so you can break them like an artist.
—Pablo Picasso

ONE THING THAT I admired about the Kenyan educational system that I went through as I was growing up was the exposure to multiple areas of study. It was a holistic education that allowed me and other children to learn different languages, science subjects, mathematics, arts, and crafts.

After one year in kindergarten and seven years in primary school, one would have already started seeing the areas where one had the most significant strengths. All that remained was guidance and mentorship from one's teachers and parents to move in a direction that would determine their future careers.

It would be dishonest to suggest that everything was hanky dory. Many parents tried hard to persuade their children to focus on the subjects that would eventually lead to a career in engineering, medicine, law, and other professions that were considered respectable

During my time in primary and high school, I never came across a student who was encouraged by their parents to focus on art and crafts. These were considered subjects without a future. Therefore, many students who would have become great artists lost their appetite in the early stages of high school. In my case, I never really lost interest in art. It was one of the subjects in which I scored good grades at O-level

Perhaps one reason that art did not receive such good press was that there were no good-paying jobs for artists. There were only a few art galleries in the main cities. The people who bought works of art were mainly foreigners and tourists who had a good appreciation of the aesthetic value of works of art.

I must confess that even if I loved art, I did not quite understand why foreigners and tourists paid large sums of money for paintings, pencil drawings, and other works of art. Stories of paintings in western countries going for hundreds of thousands of dollars, or even millions of dollars, did not seem to make any sense.

However, one day in 1975, I realized in a rather unexpected way how a piece of art could acquire an almost immeasurable intrinsic value.

For the final O-level art examinations, students were required to submit two pieces of artwork: a water painting created within three hours during the examination day; and a print prepared several days earlier. And once a student handed in their work, that was it.

Students never even gave a second thought to what happened to the paintings and prints they handed in, some of which were excellent creative pieces.

In early 1975, after the examination results were announced, I noticed an error in my exam transcript. It was in my brother's name, who was one year behind me in the same school. I never got to know how such a mix-up happened. I never got to know how such a mix-up occurred.

When I first saw the error, I thought it would be a simple task to have it corrected. However, it proved to be a nightmare. It turned out that I had to engage senior officials at the Ministry of Education at Bima House, Nairobi, to have the error corrected.

After going to Bima House a few times, the receptionist asked me to see one senior lady. The lady was on one of the higher floors at Bima House, in a large beautiful office, in keeping with her status in the organization. I was shown into her office by her secretary. I was shown into her office by her secretary.

I sat down in a comfortable chair in front of the lady and started explaining my problem. And then, as I was narrating my story, I saw a print hanging on the wall behind her. The print looked familiar. Upon closer examination, I could not believe my eyes. It was the print I had handed in for my O-level art exam.

I temporarily stopped explaining my issue. I informed the lady that the print behind her was my creation. She was stunned. She said something like, "What!" She then stood up and removed the print from the wall. She checked the index number at the back of it. And wonder of wonders, the number matched my examination index number.

At that point, two exciting things happened in quick succession. The lady explained what I needed to do to get a new examination transcript with the correct name. The index number at the back of the picture went a long way in facilitating her decision on the matter. Secondly, she scrambled to find a big envelope in which to wrap the print. She handed the print to me. She said that it would be of more value to me than her. And she was right.

The lady explained that she had walked into the area where examiners were marking artwork and stumbled on my discarded print. She liked it and arranged to have it framed and hang on the wall in her office.

I could not believe what had happened. I was delighted to receive the print. Today, it is one of my most valuable possessions. It is not an exceptional work of art, but it has an intrinsic value that I cannot quantify.

That unusual event at Bima House gave me a good sense of why some works of art acquire great value over time. It is not a wonder that works of art by people like Picasso and Michelangelo are highly valued. Apart from their aesthetic beauty, it is possible that there could be an exciting, valuable story behind each of their almost priceless works of art.

Few historical figures can come even close to Michelangelo and Picasso. The collections of works by these two artists are some of the most valuable works of art in the world today. The works of art that they left behind will continue to provide aesthetic enjoyment to millions of people for many years to come.

Michelangelo

MICHELANGELO DI LODOVICO BUONARROTI SIMONI was born on March 4, 1475, at Caprese in Florence, Italy. His father was a magistrate. On the other hand, his mother stayed at home to care for Michelangelo and his four brothers.

Michelangelo's mother became very sick when Michelangelo was still a baby. The family hired a wet nurse to take care of him. The wet nurse happened to be the wife of a stonecutter.

Michelangelo was returned to his mother when he was three.

When he was a young boy, his father took him to school to learn reading, writing, and mathematics. However, Michelangelo hated schooling. His passion was in art. His father was disappointed, especially because many people considered art an inferior profession. Despite the negativity, Michelangelo was clear in his mind that art was his true passion.

He liked going to a church near his home to watch people painting. His predisposition towards art did not endear himself well to his family. They were totally against it. However, at some point, his father yielded. When Michelangelo reached the age of 12 years, his father found him an art apprenticeship in Florence.

Michelangelo stood out as a great art apprentice, albeit a little full of himself, quite stubborn, and a know-it-all. He was eventually kicked out of the workshop by his master Galendiao.

Bertoldo di Giovani, an elderly sculptor for the wealthy Florentine Medici family, had spotted Michelangelo and took him into his sculpturing enterprise as an apprentice. Michelangelo became so good that other apprentices started becoming jealous of him. At times the jealousy deteriorated into actual physical fights. But Michelangelo was not deterred. Fortunately, Lorenzo, a wealthy leading figure in Florence, had spotted his talent and managed the situation, keeping Michelangelo under his wings.[11]

Michelangelo fled from Florence to Rome when the city of Florence was attacked by Charles the Great.

He moved to Rome when he was about 25. While in Rome, Michelangelo got one of the first major commissions to develop a sculpture for the Cardinal of Rome, Cardinal Jean de Bilhere. The marble sculpture took Michelangelo two years to create. La Pieta, a 6X6 foot sculpture of Mary holding Jesus Christ on her lap after the crucifixion, became a hit. It remains a major attraction in Rome up to this day.

Later on, Michelangelo took on another major assignment in Florence, that had been abandoned by other sculptors. The work involved creating a 17 feet tall statue of David, the young heroic shepherd described in the Bible who killed the giant Goliath. The sculpture took Michelangelo three years to complete. It is a magnificent piece of art that has been a significant tourist attraction in Rome for many years up to this day.

Michelangelo is renowned for multiple other magnificent works of art, including the paintings on the Sistine Chapel ceiling; the *Madonna of Bruges*, a sculpture depicting Mary and the Christ Child; *The Torment of Saint Anthony*, his first known painting, and many others.

Pablo Picasso

PABLO DIEGO JOSÉ FRANCISCO DE Paula Juan Nepomuceno María de los Remedios Cipriano de la Santísima Trinidad Ruiz y Picasso, later known only as Pablo Picasso, was born in Malaga, Spain in October 1881. He was born in a middle-class family.

He was a confident and charming little kid, with unusually big eyes. His father, Don Hose Ruiz Blasco, was a painter and an art teacher, a great role model for Picasso. When he noticed that Picasso had a natural talent in drawing, he made sure that he provided Picasso with much support.

The young Picasso was uniquely gifted[12]. He watched closely as his father painted different images. The paintings were based on important themes of the day, such as doves, bullfighting scenes, and portraits. He followed his father's footsteps all along, sometimes even assisting his father to put the finishing touches to some canvasses.

Picasso developed an intense passion for painting at an early age. He had an unquenchable urge to draw almost everything that came to his sight. His drawings were impressive. His father pushed him to enhance his skills as a painter, even taking him to art school.

The first major turning point in Picasso's life happened at La Caruna, a town in the northern part of Spain, where his father had moved with the family while searching for a better paying job. When Pablo was around 14, his father asked him to finish a painting of doves. Pablo completed the assignment quickly. The quality of his work astonished his father. Picasso had done an even better job than his father. At that point, his father decided to hand all his paints, brushes, and pallet to Picasso. It was like giving the baton of art to his son.

Picasso's life as a painter moved in twists and turns over the next several years. He worked in different places, including Barcelona, Paris, and Malaga. He returned to Paris in 1904, where he spent the rest of his life.

Picasso was immensely ambitious, with high self-confidence. He was not afraid of competing against the best artists of his time, Renoir, Cezanne, Monee, Van Gogh, Matisse, and others.

The major turning point of his life as an artist happened when he was 24 years old, shortly after photography started encroaching on the art scene in a big way. He felt that he had to do something different. He decided to pursue an entirely new direction in art. His oil painting *Les Demoiselles d'Avignon*, completed in 1907, was the symbol of this turning point. This painting was inspired by masks that he saw in the Musée d'Ethnographie museum in Paris[13]. It was like a new invention in the art world. It created a revolution in painting. The painting marked the beginning of cubism. Buchholz and Zimmermann described it as follows:

> *The adventure of cubism can be understood as an experiment in which artists tried to free themselves from the mere representation of nature, though without going so far as to create wholly abstract works. A picture was no longer primarily a depiction of the world but an object in itself.*
>
> *The transformation of a subject into an image, utterly changed but having a visual logic of its own, became the point and purpose of a painting.[14]*

When some of Picasso's fellow artists saw this painting in 1907, they were horrified. Andre Derain warned Picasso that the painting was like a curse and that they would find Picasso hanging under it one day.[15]

The transition to cubism marked a significant step towards Picasso's popularity as a painter, with his paintings attracting ever higher prices, which, in turn, triggered a turnaround in his financial position.

Cubism also spawned other modern forms of art such as collage and assemblage. Picasso continued pushing his ideas to new spheres, including creating three-dimensional pieces. It was artistic freedom and creativity at its best.[16]

Pablo Picasso died of heart complications in April 1973 when he and his wife were entertaining guests at dinner. He died at the ripe age of 91.

CHAPTER 3

Business

When everything seems to be going against you,
remember that the airplane takes off against the wind,
not with it.
—Henry Ford

MY FATHER SPENT MANY YEARS working as a civil servant in the government. He was a dedicated civil servant with hardly any interest in business. He got a job in the public service when Kenya was just coming out of the birth pangs of independence, at which time working for the government was considered an essential patriotic duty.

My father hardly talked about business, and for many years I assumed that he had never tried his hand in business, but I was wrong. When I was in secondary school, I heard him narrating a story about a business venture he had got into several years earlier. He had got into a partnership with three other friends and set up a bar and restaurant not very far from where we lived at a place called Center, next to Baharini

Primary School, Nakuru. The bar became very popular. It was always full of people in the evenings and on weekends.

However, despite the excellent patronage by customers, my father and the other partners were hardly making any profits. The business continued running for several months, but there was no change in the level of profitability.

My father could not understand what was going on. Something was just not right in terms of the business model. The revenues from the business did not seem to reflect the large number of people who were patronizing the place almost every day.

Upon some investigation, my father discovered that two of the partners running the bar on a day-by-day basis were manipulating the inventory. They would buy only a small stock for the partnership and a large inventory for their clandestine side business. So, when customers ordered drinks, they would be served with drinks from the side business's stock. Only a few customers would receive drinks from the legitimate inventory of the partnership.

So, in effect, two parallel businesses were going on. One, an extremely lucrative business with high sales turnover and almost zero overheads. The other one is a mediocre business with low sales turnover but which absorbed the two businesses' overhead costs. When my father discovered this ploy, he was livid. The matter came to the fore, and the partnership disintegrated.

My father used to make fun of the fact that after the collapse of the bar business, the unscrupulous partners set up a clothing shop at a town called Bahati, not far from Nakuru. And shortly after the clothing shop became operational, there was a burglary one night during which thieves stole all the inventory. My father used to say that the robbery was perhaps divine punishment for the theft that these individuals had perpetrated over an extended period in the bar enterprise.

But despite the many shortcomings that confront many business ventures, the business world is full of people who have genuinely made a significant impact in the world. One person, in particular, stands out as a true legendary hero, Henry Ford.

Henry Ford completely revolutionized the world of business through innovative mass production techniques. His impact became legendary.

Henry Ford

HENRY FORD WAS BORN IN rural Michigan on a family farm in July 1893. He wrote later in his life that he never really liked living in rural areas. He did not like going to school either.

When I started reading about Henry Ford, one of my most surprising discoveries was that he dropped out of school in 8th grade when he was only 15 years old.[17] This is quite incredible when one considers the nature of his subsequent forays in the business world.

Henry Ford had a passion for mechanical objects, an interest that started at an early age. Historians say that when he was 15 years old, he was given a watch by his father. He dismantled the watch, then re-assembled it meticulously. He did the same thing for watches of neighbors, earning himself a reputation as an expert watch repairer.

He left the farm when he was 16 and moved to Detroit. He worked there briefly as an apprentice in mechanical workshops. He returned to the farm when he was 19. By that time, he had gained skills as a machinist. He set up an excellent workshop on the farm.

He married Clara Bryant when he was 25 and subsequently left the farm permanently when he was around 28. He joined the Edison Illuminating Company (renamed Detroit Edison

Company later on). He was a good worker. He was promoted to Chief Engineer after only four years when he was just 31.

It is amazing to learn that Henry Ford spent a lot of his spare time building a motor vehicle with an internal combustion engine. I find it hard to put my head around this particular fact. How does a school dropout spend time building an automobile? He has to be a special kind of a school dropout, one with enormous passion and drive for mechanical objects.

Ford's interest and devotion to building automobiles did not endear him well to his employer. However, he was unfazed and decided to follow his passion. Accordingly, in 1899 he left his job to form his own company, the Detroit Automobile Company. Unfortunately, the venture was unsuccessful. His next venture was unsuccessful too.

In 1903, with the help of financial backing from Malcomson and others, Henry Ford set up the Ford Motor Company. His strategy was to mass-produce cheap cars. This strategy worked well, generating enormous profits for the Ford Motor Company.

The competitive landscape for motor cars was quite intense, but Henry Ford was unrelenting. He fought extended court battles related to patents, but this did not diminish his spirits.

A significant turning point of his business was his decision to produce a black $ 850 car, the Model T. The average price for a small car at the time was $ 2,000. He sold the vehicle by the thousands, lifting the Ford Motor Company into one of America's largest car manufacturers.

He perfected mass production techniques at low cost. Ironically, he did this while paying the industry's highest wage rate ($5 per hour). It was part of a profit-sharing plan. Some said that this was the most foolish thing ever done by an industrialist. But Henry Ford had a different view. The high wage would not only increase the income of the workers, but the workers would also become buyers of the Model T, which would create a virtuous cycle for the company. It would also enable the company to reduce turnover and retain good staff.

By 1913 the Ford Motor Company had innovated in the production process using an assembly line. It was churning out 1,000 cars a day.

By the end of 2019, the Ford Motor Company had a market capitalization of US$ 38.0 billion[18]. The company had 10,921 dealerships worldwide, with sales of 5.4 million cars in 2019, and a workforce of 190,000 employees. The value of the company's total assets was US$ 258.5 billion[19].

To cut a long story short, a high school dropout with a passion for building motor cars built a company that, in only 100 years, would become an industrial giant. Henry Ford became one of the most influential people in America. Unfortunately, money and power got into his mind, transforming him into a different individual. Some thought that he had become a tyrant who believed that the world revolved around him. But that part of Henry Ford's life is out of scope for our present purposes.

Henry Ford's meteoric rise to greatness was an amazing part of his life and is the focus of our attention. He was a major player in revolutionizing industrial production, an incredible fit.

CHAPTER 4

Economics

*The difficulty lies not so much in developing new ideas
as in escaping from old ones.*
—*John Maynard Keynes*

WHEN I THINK ABOUT ECONOMICS, the first thing that usually comes to my mind is optimization. For many years, I have held the view that almost everything in life is about optimization. In other words, we are all continually trying to look for a balance among competing demands. And it starts from the trivialities of personal life to the large-scale global aspects of our lives.

For example, when I was a small boy, I remember how we loved sugary things yet never seemed to get enough of them. My mum would buy enough sugar for breakfast tea. And sure enough, everyone would put the required two tea spoonful's in their cup of tea. Anyone who tried to break this rule would most likely get something else that was always plentiful in supply, namely pulling of the cheeks or ears. And in the worst-case scenario, they would get at least two ngotos (a knock on the head with the back of the middle finger).

Not only was my mum intent on making sure that we lived a healthy balanced life, but there was the family budget that she needed to optimize

Of course, wherever there are rules, there are those whose mantra is to break them. I have often heard it said that "rules are made to be broken." One of my sisters was one of those who believed in this mantra, especially in sugar-related matters. One day, when she was about 12 years old, she woke up at night when everybody else in the family was asleep. She walked into the kitchen stealthily and opened the kitchen cupboard where my mum kept sugar. The sugar was in a brown khaki packet. My sister's idea was simple. She would just put her hand into the pack and scoop as much sugar as she could. She would then slowly walk back to her bed and enjoy the sweetness in between the blankets while everybody else was asleep.

My sister's scheme worked exceptionally well. However, just as she was about to scoop the sugar from the packet, a huge rat jumped out of one corner of the cupboard. She screamed at the top of her voice, waking up everybody in the house.

There was total panic, as nobody knew what had happened. My sister was just crying uncontrollably. She then explained that a rat had tried to attack her.

A few minutes later, it emerged that the rat attacked my sister as she was "taking" some sugar from the cupboard. Everyone was full of pity, and many cursed the "damn" rat, but they all knew tacitly that they had just witnessed someone paying a high price for their sins.

My mum may have had a separate secret conversation with my sister the following morning regarding the consequences of trying to optimize a system by taking shortcuts. We see this kind of phenomenon in different forms every day.

On a much larger scale, we have seen what sometimes happens when a nation makes a significant effort to allocate resources optimally. An unscrupulous individual then decides to siphon some of the funds for their selfish personal use.

The reader may find these examples of optimization simplistic and even humorous. Still, the examples help illustrate ideas that economists have grappled with during the past two centuries.

At the heart of economics is the study of the invisible forces of supply and demand in different contexts. These forces eventually reach an equilibrium, independently or through external intervention.

And as in almost every discipline, there are times in history when an individual walks onto the stage and radically changes the conventional wisdom. Charles Darwin did it in evolutionary science, Isaac Newton did it in physics, and Albert Einstein did it in physics. John Maynard Keynes did it in economics, helping to steer the destinies of many western nations.

Keynesian economic theories may no longer have the potency that they had in the 1930s. Still, the indelible mark that was left by Keynes is evident up to this day.

The prosperity of a country depends to a large extent on the sound economic management by its leaders. Indeed, the economy is usually the central theme in any political campaign for election to high office in a country. And yet, economics is riddled with fuzziness. To quote Henry Hazlitt[20]:

> *Economics is haunted by more fallacies than any other study known to man. This is no accident. The inherent difficulties of the subject would be great enough in any case, but they are multiplied a thousand-fold by a factor that is insignificant in, say, physics, mathematics, or medicine – the special pleading of selfish interests.*

HISTORICAL SNAPSHOTS OF THE GREAT

Hazlitt's sentiments can perhaps be better appreciated when one considers that one of the fundamental aspects of economic policy is the allocation and management of a country's scarce resources. So, different people would wish to pursue the line of thought and articulation of economic theory and policy that best suits their interests. This means that everything presented as an economic policy needs to be consumed with a pinch of salt.

However, from time to time, an individual has emerged with novel non-partisan ideas that have helped policymakers and practitioners to steer a country in the right direction. Examples of such individuals include Adam Smith (1723-1790), whose book, "The Wealth of Nations," is considered the first modern economics work. August von Hayek (1899 – 1992), whose pioneering work on the theory of money and other related concepts, earned him the 1974 Nobel Memorial Prize in Economic Sciences. Another example is John Maynard Keynes, who is considered the father of macroeconomics.

Several other individuals have had a significant influence on economics too. Still, the three examples cited here are some of the biggest giants in the field. We will focus on Keynes, whose influence in the post-World War I years was legendary. Indeed, his theories and policy prescriptions are still valid today.

John Maynard Keynes

JOHN MAYNARD KEYNES WAS BORN into a middle-class family in Cambridge, United Kingdom, on June 5, 1883. His father was a senior administrator at Cambridge University.

He studied at the prestigious Eton College and subsequently joined the equally prestigious University of Cambridge in 1902. He pursued a degree in mathematics. One of his professors convinced him to pursue economics at the higher graduate level.

He excelled in economics. However, it was only in his mid-30s when he made a significant mark in the discipline, after writing the book entitled "The General Theory of Employment, Interest, and Money."

He became a celebrity. But what is it that made Keynes so famous?

Ever since the time of the other enormously influential economist, Adam Smith, it was believed by economists that the forces of supply and demand generally determined price levels. These classical ideas were straightforward and easy to understand.

To put it simplistically, the idea was that if the demand for goods and services in an economy went up, then the prices of goods would go up too. In other words, there would be too much money chasing too few goods, meaning that producers of the goods and services would want to cash in by raising the prices of their goods and services.

The converse was also correct. If the quantity of goods and services went up, then consumers would bargain for lower prices. This phenomenon would occur because producers would be jostling amongst themselves, trying to get consumers to buy their goods.

According to classical economic theory, these forces of demand and supply would work against each other until they reached a natural equilibrium level. In other words, the optimal level where both consumers and producers were happy to operate over a given period. This is the so-called dogma of letting market forces determine market prices.

Classical economists believed that the government should not interfere with market forces because market forces were efficient and would settle at the most natural and optimal level. In other words, the economy operates on some kind of auto-pilot.

This is putting things in very simplistic terms. For instance, as you ponder about this classical theory, just remember that it refers to aggregates. In other words, when we talk about prices, we are referring not only to the prices of goods and services but also to general wage levels (i.e., prices of labor).

Then, in comes Keynes!

Keynes argued that while the classical theory was correct, it was only valid in the long run. In other words, the equilibrium of prices and supply would realistically take far too long, and as he famously said: "in the long run, we will all be dead." This meant that when a country was going through a recession, it would take far too long for the economy to adjust to the right level. Accordingly, Keynes argued, government intervention was required in such situations to bring things back on course in the short run. And the best course of action was for the government to increase investment, even if the investment necessitated borrowing to stimulate production and raise demand. Such deliberate government action would reduce unemployment and also trigger positive multiplier effects in the economy.

Keynes's ideas were revolutionary. He was in effect saying that in times of economic hardship in a country, the government should not cut spending as intuition would suggest. Instead, the government should increase the level of spending to stimulate the economy.

Keynes's ideas were tried successfully in various countries, changing the economic well-being of billions of people.

Here is an example to illustrate the application of Keynesian ideas. During the Great Depression that followed the stock market crash of 1929, President Franklin D Roosevelt of the USA responded by implementing the New Deal. The New Deal was a series of programs, public work projects, financial reforms, and regulations.

The construction of the Hoover Dam between 1931 and 1936 was one of the projects in the New Deal. The development of the dam was a massive project. The project created direct employment for 5,000 workers and many other indirect jobs. This included jobs for businesses that supplied construction materials to the project, as well as other contractors. It also created jobs for other people on whom the workers on the project depended for different types of services.

A new city, Boulder City, emerged, with grocery stores, schools, and many other facilities. Many more multiplier effects contributed to the stimulation of the economy of the United States.

Keynes had several critics. People who did not believe that it was right for the government to interfere with market forces. However, none of them wholly invalidated Keynes's theories.

Indeed, even as late as 2008, governments were still pursuing Keynesian policies. For example, after the stock market crash in 2008, the United States government spent billions of dollars to stimulate the economy rather than cutting back on spending.

It is truly mind-boggling to note that just one person, John Maynard Keynes, could have such a significant impact on billions of people worldwide. It is truly phenomenal.

CHAPTER 5

Exploration

*You can never cross the ocean unless you have the
courage to lose sight of the shore.*
— *Christopher Columbus*

WHEN I WAS ABOUT TEN years old, I looked forward to weekends because these were the times that I would spend with other kids playing different types of games.

The game we played was dependent on the season. For example, during the hot, dry season, we would spend most of the day flying kites. Occasionally, we would build catapults and spend the day bird hunting.

Bird hunting was my first introduction to exploration. We would start by looking for birds near our home. Our hunting escapades would sometimes extend for several miles from our home – but we did not realize how far we were until it was time to return home.

I remember vividly one kid named Kiguta, who was truly exceptional. He was not content with looking for birds in the area near our home. He pushed other kids to travel far, sometimes as far as Lake Nakuru, looking for birds.

We would spend hours in the forest around Lake Nakuru, where there were plenty of birds. At that time, the forest had not been converted into a game park.

When I reflect on our escapades, I wonder how we never encountered wild animals. Children do indeed have special protection from God.

Were it not for Kiguta's drive for exploration far from our familiar neighborhood, our hunting missions would not have been as bountiful as they proved to be. It is this kind of spirit of exploration that led to the discovery of America by Christopher Columbus and the opening up of trade routes from Europe to India by Vasco da Gama.

Christopher Columbus

CHRISTOPHER COLUMBUS WAS BORN IN Genoa, Italy. There is no definite record of his birth date, but historians believe that he was born in 1451. He was born in a family of modest means. Still, historical records show that he lived a healthy life without any hardships.

He did not have any formal education. He left home when he was around 20 years old and spent time doing different jobs related to the sea. He traveled extensively and, over time, developed skills as a seaman and gained a lot of knowledge in map reading.

He was determined to discover a new route to the east by sailing westwards. He studied maps and other literature and eventually concluded that he could reach his destination by sailing westwards for 3,000 miles.

He lobbied extensively for resources to make the journey but met with negative responses most of the time. In 1485, he reached out to the King of Portugal, King John II. The King asked a team of experts to review Columbus's proposal. The experts rejected the proposal because Columbus's estimate of the distance that he proposed to travel was far too low. He made a second attempt to the King in 1488. His bid was not successful, mainly because his brother, Bartolomeu Diaz, had discovered an alternative route to the Far East via the Cape of Good Hope in southern Africa.

Columbus also presented his proposals in Genoa and Venice without much luck. He reached out to King Henry VII in England, too, but did not succeed either.

In 1486, he presented his proposals to the monarchs of Aragon and Castille, Ferdinand II and Isabella I, respectively.

They did not accept the proposal (Aragon and Castile joined together to form Spain in 1479).

After two years of negotiations, Queen Isabella I and King Ferdinand II finally agreed to sponsor the voyage. The Queen and the King agreed primarily because they were keen to prevent Columbus from getting sponsorship from another ruler.

The rewards that the monarchy promised Columbus on the successful completion of the voyage were enormous. Firstly, he would be appointed Admiral of the Ocean Sea, and Viceroy and Governor of all the new territories that he could claim for Spain. Further, he would have the privilege of nominating three people for any office in the new territories, from whom the monarch could select one. He would have a perpetual entitlement to 10% of all the revenues from the new territories. In addition, would have the right to buy a 12.5% interest in any commercial venture in the new territories and 12.5% of profits from all such enterprises.

Columbus set off on his journey on August 3rd, 1492. He set sail aboard the *Santa Maria*, accompanied by two other smaller vessels, *La Pinta*, and *La Nina* piloted by Martín Alonso Pinzón and Vicente Yáñez Pinzón respectively.

The first stop was at the Canary Islands on August 9th, 1492, the southwestern extremity of the Spanish territory. When the crew was ready to continue on the expedition, he gave them only one instruction, "just sail westwards on a straight line." It was a journey that required enormous courage as no one knew, for sure, whether they would reach the destination after traveling for 3,000 miles, as estimated by Christopher Columbus. The team set sail on September 6th, 1492.

On October 10th, 1492, after sailing for about four weeks, the people in the expedition started becoming restless. They gave Christopher Columbus an ultimatum that if they did not see land in the next three days, they would turn back and return to Spain. Christopher Columbus assured them that the land was not far away. Eventually, they did sight land. They landed in the Bahamas on October 12th, 1492.

Columbus's primary objective was to discover the sources of gold and spices. He did not find the sources but was able to obtain some gold from an Indian Chief called Waganagari.

He sailed back to Spain with the gold, slaves, and other goods from the new lands.

He made three more trips to the Americas. The second trip in September 1493 comprised 17 ships carrying 1,200 people, including priests, farmers, and soldiers. The third trip in May 1498 was a little less grandiose. He sailed with six ships.

Unfortunately, the people he had carried as settlers during his second voyage revolted because they did not find the riches he had promised them. He returned to Spain in disgrace, as a prisoner. The Spanish monarchy even stripped him of the title of Governor. He was later released.

He made his fourth voyage in May 1502, in the company of his 13-year-old son Fernando and his brother Bartolomeo.

His final days of exploration were full of controversy. The monarchy reneged on the contract with Columbus. Christopher Columbus also landed into trouble with the monarchy in Spain, spending many years in court.

Christoper Columbus passed away in Spain on May 20th, 1506.

The controversy around Columbus's remains is a long story. His remains were moved from place to place, finally landing at Seville in Spain. Interestingly, there are other remains in San Domingo, in the Dominican Republic, that are said to belong to him too. So, the controversy around one of the greatest explorers in the world still lives on.

During his voyages to the Americas, the brutality that Christopher Columbus meted out to the natives that he found there was beyond measure and put a big blemish on his reputation.

However, despite all the unfortunate shenanigans with the monarchy, and the divergent opinions amongst historians on his impact on indigenous Americans, he is the man who showed the Europeans the path to America.

Ironically, America was named after Amerigo Vespucci, an Italian explorer who arrived on the continent after Columbus.

Vasco da Gama

THE PRECISE DATE OF VASCO da Gama's birth is not known. Historians believe that he was born in 1460 or 1469.

Vasco da Gama was born in Sines in Portugal in a family of humble nobility. He was the third born in a family of six children - five boys and one girl. Details of his early life are scanty, with some historians believing that he studied navigation and mathematics at the town of Evora. Not much else is known about his education.

He was the first European explorer to discover the sea route to India via the southern tip of Africa. The use of this route enabled Portugal to avoid the more dangerous route via the Mediterranean Sea. King John III of Portugal sponsored his first voyage.

One of the exciting aspects of Da Gama's trip was that upon arrival in the Cape Verde Islands, he decided to take an unconventional route for his onward journey. Rather than following the traditional route via the coast of Africa, he proceeded in a southern direction in the open seas, sailing for three months without any sight of land. Using a different route was an amazing feat that required tremendous courage. He arrived in Calicut, India, in May 1498, ten months after his departure from Lisbon, Portugal.

Vasco da Gama's focus on India was driven by a desire to access spices, mainly pepper and cinnamon.

He started his return trip on August 14, 1498. He defied advice from people who were knowledgeable about the Indian ocean. Because of this, he encountered significant challenges on his return journey, during which he lost several sailors.

Vasco da Gama arrived on the coast of East Africa with a damaged ship. Also, he took four times as long to travel from India as he had done in the outward journey. The remainder of the trip back to Portugal was uneventful, arriving in Lisbon on August 29, 1499, with only one-third of his original crew.

People in Portugal were elated by the news of Vasco Da Gama's return from India. He received various rewards from the King of Portugal, including a hereditary lordship and entitlement to a handsome annual payment.

HISTORICAL SNAPSHOTS OF THE GREAT

Vasco da Gama's second trip to India was characterized by political antagonism with the local political leaders. The intrigues eventually deteriorated into acts of brutality and atrocities of unimaginable proportions. In one particular incident, wishing to exert revenge on Muslims who had opposed the establishment of a Portuguese factory in India, he captured a ship carrying 700 Muslim pilgrims heading to Mecca. He had all the 700 people locked up in the ship's lower decks and had the ship set ablaze. It was a horrifying act of brutality and was only one amongst a host of other acts of extreme cruelty perpetrated by Vasco da Gama.

Vasco da Gama opened up the sea routes from Europe to India, enabling the Portuguese to gain a foothold in a vast colonial empire in Asia. Other European nations followed about a century later, notably Netherlands, England, France, and Denmark.

CHAPTER 6

Literature

All the world's a stage, and all the men and women
merely players: they have their exits and their
entrances; and one man in his time plays many parts,
his acts being seven ages.
—*William Shakespeare*

WHEN I THINK OF ENGLISH literature, it reminds me of an incident in High School that some of my schoolmates never seem to forget.

When we were in Form 3, we learned that one student in Form 4, let's call him Kamau, had created a stir in the literature class. The Form 4 students had just come from a chemistry class. During that class, the teacher had performed an experiment that ended with a minor explosion. The explosion was so mesmerizing that the students could hardly stop talking about it even as the teacher tried to explain the science behind it. One of the things that the chemistry teacher said was that the explosion was due to a dubious phenomenon.

When the chemistry lesson ended, the students moved from the laboratory to another classroom for an English literature lesson. Upon arrival in the classroom, the teacher asked the students to write a short essay. Kamau started his essay with the words: "Due to dubious phenomenon and faragages….."

Later on, the contents of Kamau's essay were revealed. It was a hilarious essay, not because of its content, but because of English language phrases that could only compete with those of William Shakespeare. From that day on, students nick-named Kamau "Dubious Phenomenon." The name stuck. Now, I cannot even remember his real name.

WE MAY LAUGH AT DUBIOUS PHENOMENON, but the truth is that the writings of many literary figures who have risen to fame can hardly be understood by an average person.

The legal profession is perhaps one where language has taken a life of its own. You just need to read any standard contract. In some instances, you would be superhuman if you did not get a migraine after reading two pages. Take the following extract from Section 37 of The Landlord and Tenant Bill, 2007 - Kenya Law:

37 (1) Where any sum has been paid on account of any rent, being a sum which is, under this Act, irrecoverable by the landlord, the sum so paid shall be recoverable from the landlord who received payment, or from the landlord's legal or personal representative, by the tenant by whom it was paid, and any such sum, and any other sum which under the provisions of this Act is recoverable by a tenant from a landlord or payable or repayable by a landlord to a tenant, may, without prejudice to any other method of recovery, be deducted by the tenant from any rent payable by the tenant to the landlord.

Two questions immediately pop up in one's mind after reading this "sentence." Why do lawyers hate the full stop so much? Would using a full stop be a misdemeanor, a felony, or similar crime that the legal fraternity deems inconsistent with the interests of the legal profession or otherwise prejudicial to the interests of lawyers who would otherwise find it difficult to find work that involves drafting almost incomprehensible legal documents and other supporting documents that are essential for defending the interests of a particular party in the court of law in whom the lawyer in question expects a decent fee to sustain the said lawyer for a duration at least ten times the duration that the lawyer spends in court defending the said party thereof or ten consecutive days whichever is lower?

Philosophers are also notorious for incomprehensible literature. I look forward to the day when I will meet someone who can explain it to me in plain English Martin Heidegger's 590-page volume "*Being and Time: First Half.*"

However, some individuals have come onto the scene and completely mesmerized people with their literary prowess. They include the English playwright and poet William Shakespeare, the English romantic poet Percy Bysshe Shelley, and the Norwegian playwright and theatre director Henrik Johan Ibsen. Others include Nobel Prize laureate Wole Soyinka and Kenyan writer and academic Ngugi wa Thiong'o. All these individuals have lived interesting lives, driven by a certain unique artistic energy. We will briefly explore the lives of two of them, William Shakespeare and Percy Bysshe Shelley.

William Shakespeare

WILLIAM SHAKESPEARE WAS BORN IN Stratford-upon-Avon on April 26, 1564, to a relatively prosperous family. His father was a businessman. His mother was the daughter of a landowner.

The history of his early education and early life is scanty. Historical records indicate that he left school at the age of 13. It turns out his father was unable to pay school fees due to financial problems brought about by a massive fine due to illegal trading in wool.

William Shakespeare married Anne Hathaway when he was only 18. Anne was eight years older than him.

HISTORICAL SNAPSHOTS OF THE GREAT

William Shakespeare moved to London in 1585 when he was 21. He spent a lot of his time in theatres there, writing plays and acting. He wrote prolifically, initially starting with comedy and history, subsequently migrating to tragedies.

Some of his early works include the comedies *"Much Ado About Nothing," "A Midsummer's Night Dream,"* and the tragedies *"Hamlet," "Othello,"* and *"King Lear."* All these were excellent works that received much critical acclaim in literary circles of the day. During his lifetime, he wrote 154 sonnets and 38 plays. He died on April 23, 1616, three days before his 52nd birthday.

Samuel Taylor Coleridge said the following of Shakespeare:

> *Shakespeare, no mere child of nature; no automaton of genius; no passive vehicle of inspiration possessed by the spirit, not possessing it; first studied patiently, meditated deeply, understood minutely, till knowledge became habitual and intuitive, wedded itself to his habitual feelings, and at length gave birth to that stupendous power by which he stands alone, with no equal or second in his own class; to that power which seated him on one of the two glorysmitten summits of the poetic mountain, with Milton's his compeer, not rival.*

The demand for plays was extremely high. Accordingly, Shakespeare spent most of his time during the day acting in the theatre and spent time in the evening writing. The only exception to this routine was during lent when play-acting was forbidden.

He appears to have had a strange love life. Some historians believe that he was in love with the Earl of Southampton, perhaps explaining why he spent so much time in London away from his wife. This assumption is supported by the many sonnets that he wrote addressed to a male lover.

Shakespeare's plays are replete with darkness and death, perhaps reflecting the bubonic plague that was killing people in England at the time.

The death of his 11-year old only son, Hamlet, in August 1596 was devastating. There was no son to inherit his wealth. That meant that the name Shakespeare would disappear irrespective of the amount of wealth that he inherited. Historians believe that his deep feelings for his son inspired his play "Hamlet." The famous line "to be, or not to be, that is the question" comes from *"Hamlet."*

Some historians believe that in 1610 when William Shakespeare was 46, he may have been one of the collaborators in translating the Bible from Latin into the English King James version. The indirect evidence used by some historians to support this claim is that if you count 46 words from the beginning of Psalms 46, you will find the word "shake." Similarly, if you count the 46 words from the end of Psalms 46, you will find the word "spear." This is a bizarre way of reasoning, but some believed that it was an indirect way of William Shakespeare putting his signature on part authorship of the King James Version of the Bible. There was even speculation that he wrote the entire King James Version of the Bible.

At some point in his career, Shakespeare faced opposition from the city fathers who did not want to renew leases for the land where the theatre stood. They considered plays as un-Godly and immoral entertainment. They brought down the theatre, but Shakespeare was not deterred in his determination. He used the wooden planks of the destroyed theatre to build a new theatre in the seedy side of south London, among the gambling houses, brothels, and other unseemly establishments.

The first theatre was called the Globe Theatre, in which he held a 10% interest. His first play in that theatre was *Julius Caesar*. Because of the modest nature of the theatre, he made up for the shortcomings of the infrastructure with language. He participated in the plays that he had written, but not as the main actor.

The quality of his writing grew over time. In his later years, he wrote some of the greatest dramas in his career, including the tragedies *Othello, Macbeth*, and *King Lear*. His last play was "*The Tempest.*"

The Global Theatre burned down accidentally in 1613 during the performance of "*William the VIII,*" bringing Shakespeare's career to an end.

He returned to Stratford on retirement as a wealthy man. A new theatre was built but without his involvement.

In his Will, he left his wife Anna Hathaway, "the second-best bed and the furniture," an indication perhaps of a sore relationship with her before his death.

His works were compiled by his fellow actors 11 years after his death, led by his severest critic and friend Ben Johnson. Without this effort, we would never have known of the great works of Shakespeare.

Some writers have said that the high quality of William Shakespeare's writing can be attributed to his deep understanding of the human condition.

Percy Bysshe Shelley

PERCY BYSSHE SHELLEY STANDS OUT as one of the most unusual characters in the history of English literature. He was born in a relatively well to do family, educated in good schools, but grew into a radical figure in academic, social, and political circles. He was a thorn in the flesh of the political establishment, right up to the end of his short life of 29 years. Ironically, after his death, even those who hated him when he was alive paid tribute to his enormous intellect and influence in English poetry and political philosophy.

Percy Bysshe Shelley was born in Sussex, England, on August 4, 1792. His father was a Member of Parliament, and his mother, the daughter of a landowner in Sussex. He was the eldest in a family of six children: four sisters and one brother. The available literature suggests that he had an enjoyable life as a youngster, spending a lot of time fishing and hunting.

He started his schooling at Syon House Academy in Brentford and subsequently moved to the prestigious Eton College. He was subjected to a lot of bullying while at Eton. The incidents affected him psychologically, turning him into a taciturn loner who did not like participating in games and other social activities. But that notwithstanding, he had a naughty side to him. His final act at Eton was to blow up a tree using gun powder.

Shelly joined University College, Oxford, in April 1810. He was a strange student. He attended only one lecture, spending the rest of the time reading books of his choice.

He published three works during his first year at Oxford. The first one was a novel entitled "*Zastrozzi: A Romance,*" which he had started writing when he was at Eton College. One literary critic described the main character in the book as "one of the most savage and improbable demons that ever issued from a diseased brain." This novel perhaps ought to have sent a message on the kind of individual that Shelly was to become in later years.

His second novel was entitled "*St. Irvyne; or, The Rosicrucian: A Romance,*" a horror novel. The third publication was "*Original Poetry by Victor and Cazire,*" a compilation of 16 poems, co-written with his sister Elizabeth. However, this last book became problematic after publication because it contained a poem by Matthew Lewis. Shelly suppressed the publication of the book for fear of a plagiarism lawsuit. He told the publisher that his sister was the one who had included the poem in the book.

In 1811, Oxford expelled Shelly for publishing a pamphlet that was considered heretical. The pamphlet was entitled "*The Necessity of Atheism.*" His father intervened, and the university authorities agreed to re-admit Shelly on the condition that he recanted his views on atheism. Shelly refused to recant his views, and that was the end of education at Oxford.

Four months after leaving Oxford, Shelly, who was 19 then, married Harriet Westbrook, a 16-year old girl. His father had forbidden him from seeing this girl, so the marriage did not go down well with his father.

In 1812, Shelly traveled to Dublin, Ireland. While there, he published an extremely seditious article entitled "*Address to the Irish People.*" In the article, he highlighted the evils of the state. He also prescribed the action that Irish people needed to take to correct the situation, including a repeal of the Union Act.

Shelly's love life was full of trouble and intrigue. He was in love with his cousin when he married Harriet. When he moved in with Harriet, he asked his friend Hogg to join them. Hogg made advances to Harriet and was thrown out. While married to Harriet, Shelly was seeing a 28-year old school teacher. His relationship with Harriet became strained, forcing her to move back to her parent's home. In July 1814, Shelly abandoned Harriet, who had become pregnant. He moved to Switzerland with Mary, the daughter of William Godwin, along with her sister, but returned to England six weeks later.

Harriet committed suicide in December 1816 while pregnant. Shelly subsequently married Mary. The court ordered that Shelly's children with Harriet be given to foster parents on account of Shelly's atheism and his abandonment of his first wife.

In 1818 Shelly's infant daughter passed away. This was followed by the illness and death of his son in 1818. He lost another baby daughter in 1820.

During the years 1817 and 1822, Shelly wrote controversial poems attacking religion and the political establishment.

Shelly died in 1822 through drowning. But there was some speculation that he was murdered for political reasons or by some of his debtors. There was a third theory that a robber killed him.

Percy left a rich legacy in poetry and offered inspiration to numerous literary scholars, some of whom became literary giants in their own right. The list of his works is extensive.

CHAPTER 7

Monarchy

Conquering the world on horseback is easy; it is
dismounting and governing that is hard.
— *Genghis Khan*

MY FIRST PERSONAL ENCOUNTER WITH monarchy was in 1969, at, amongst all places, Jamhuri Estate, Nairobi. Indeed, I lived near a King for several months before the King decided to move to another location.

I never saw the King again, but he left a lasting impression in my mind. He was the tallest human being I had ever seen. He radiated a unique kind of confidence that I assumed only came from a member of the monarchy.

What I never quite reconciled in my mind, however, was just how such an important member of society could reside in Jamhuri Estate. What was his role as a King, I wondered? And what did it take to become a King?

Although I filled some of these mental gaps with the history that I learned in High School, the puzzle in my mind has never been fully resolved. But I know that there are members of the monarchy who have done great things for humanity.

IN 1969, MY FATHER DECIDED TO RELOCATE the family from Nakuru to Nairobi. Our new home was at Jamhuri Estate, on the south-western side of Nairobi, about four kilometers from the Nairobi Central Business District. Moving from Nakuru to Nairobi was an immensely traumatic experience for me, mainly because I lost all my close friends literally overnight. In fact, since that time, slightly over 50 years ago, I met my best childhood friends Kanja, Gitaka, and Warui, only once.

When I visited Nakuru in 2019, I was surprised to learn that Kanja had apparently joined the Kenya Navy several years earlier, rising to the position of captain, and had just retired.

The picture of Kanja, the kid, in retirement, did not quite register in my mind properly. It was as if my mind was still suspended in the distant memory of my days as a kid growing up in Nakuru. It was incredible. But that was the stuff of life.

So, when we moved from Nakuru to Jamhuri Estate in 1969, I had to start building friendships all over again. It was not easy. Jamhuri Estate was a relatively new housing estate. People were moving in from different parts of the city as we were settling down.

I made a few friends, but the closeness of our relationship was nowhere near the bond that I had built with Kanja, Gitaka, Warui, and other friends in Nakuru.

Strangely, many of the people I became attached to were the domestic workers in the neighborhood. I remember vividly one particular worker, John, who never seemed to run out of stories. Other workers and children in the neighborhood seemed to gravitate around him. He seemed to know everything that was happening in the area: who was moving in, where he came from, the number of people in his or her family, where he or she worked, and other unique insights on the person's behavior.

Nobody seemed to question the truth of John's information. Most of the information was quite juicy. We preferred not to ask too many questions lest John lost enthusiasm for sharing the exciting insights.

On one particular occasion, John told us that a certain King from Rwanda had moved into the neighborhood. I remember being almost overwhelmed by the strangeness of that piece of information.

John said that the King was an exceptionally tall gentleman from the Hutu tribe in Rwanda and that the King had moved to Kenya on exile from Rwanda. How John had gathered that information will forever remain a mystery.

Initially, I doubted what John was saying until I saw the Rwandan King. If his height was an indication of Kingliness, then John was right. The King was the tallest man I had ever seen in my life. No wonder he was a King, so I thought.

A few months later, the King left Jamhuri Estate, presumably for Rwanda. So, I can claim confidently that for several months during the year 1969, I lived in the same neighborhood as a King. But what I never quite understood was why some people became Kings and what Kings, or the monarchy, really did. I would learn some of these things in high school. And I am still learning.

One common feature of the people who one could refer to as great members of the monarchy was the brutality that they visited upon other human beings. The monarchy committed some of the worst atrocities known to humanity. We will explore a few examples.

Biography Online lists several members of the monarchy who were influential over the ages. They include the Egyptian pharaoh Ramesses the Great (c. 1279 – 1213 BC), the King of Macedonia Alexander the Great (c. 356 – 323 BC), and Julius

Caesar (c. 100 to 44 BC), the Roman ruler who set himself up as the sole dictator of Rome after overthrowing the leadership of the Roman Republic but who was eventually murdered by senators. Others are Augustus Ceaser (c. 63 – 14 BC), the adopted son of Julius Ceaser who became the first Roman Emperor after the murder of Julius Ceaser, Marcus Aurelius (121 – 180 AD) who was considered a just and wise Roman Emperor who practiced stoicism, and Emporer Constantine (c. 272 – 337 AD), the First Roman Emperor to embrace Christianity[21].

Other influential members of the monarchy include Charlemagne (c. 742 – 814), the Roman Emperor who played a significant role in strengthening the position of Christianity in Europe, William the Conqueror (c. 1028 to 1087), who successfully invaded England in 1066, becoming the first Norman King to rule England, and Saladin (1138 – 1193), leader of the Arab tribes who successfully drove out the Christian crusaders.

Others are Genghis Khan (1162 – 1227), the ruler of the Mongol Empire who left a trail of death and destruction in his military campaigns across Europe and Asia. Babur (1483 – 1531) too, a descendant of Genghis Khan, and who became ruler at the age of only 12, and who established the Mogul Empire in India. And Catherine the Great (1729 – 1796), the longest-serving Russian monarch, having ruled for 34 years.

Others are Queen Victoria (1819 – 1901), the symbol of British imperialism, and Princess Diana (1961 - 1997), an icon of the British monarchy in the 21st Century and notable for her charity work.

Of all these individuals, the three that I find fascinating as monarchs and who can give us insights on the inner motivations of monarchs are Ramesses the Great, William the Conqueror, and Genghis Khan.

Ramesses II

RAMESSES THE GREAT OR RAMESSES II was an Egyptian pharaoh who lived around 1303 – 1213 BC. He was in power for 67 years, during which he built a lot of infrastructure in Egypt, including numerous magnificent temples. He became an army captain at the age of 10 and commanded an army of more than 20,000 soldiers when he was 25 years of age.

Ramesses expanded the Egyptian Kingdom by conquering other nations in the Levant region, all the way to Canaan, and south of Egypt in Nubia, and on the western side in present-day Libya. When he died, he was buried in a tomb. Quite amazingly, his remains were discovered in 1881 and are currently on display in a museum in Egypt[22].

One of the most memorable battles he fought was in Kadesh, present-day Syria, in 1274 BC. He left Egypt with an army of 20,000 soldiers. When he approached Kadesh, he decided to attack the city from the western side with only 5,000 troops, leaving the other forces to slowly follow behind.

Upon reaching the outskirts of Kadesh, he was struck by the greenery and beauty of the place. Most importantly, it appeared that the city was unguarded, which presented him with an opportunity for a quick and easy victory. However, he was mistaken. The King of Kadesh had laid a trap on Ramesses. The King of Kadesh (King of the Hittites) had a battalion of 40,000 soldiers who quickly encircled Ramesses and his soldiers. However, in a brazen display of courage, Ramesses decided to fight the Hittites fearlessly despite being significantly outnumbered. There was no victor in the battle, but it was incredible that Ramesses did not lose despite the significant odds. The two rulers agreed on a truce, which was held for several years. (It is noteworthy that Ramesses had a harem of many wives who bore him more than 100 children.)

William the Conqueror

WILLIAM THE CONQUEROR IS ONE of the most unusual characters in the history of monarchies. He was born out of wedlock in Normandy, France. It is astounding that he subsequently became the King of England and is reputed to have caused some of the most significant changes in English history.

William's mother was Herleva, the mistress of his father Robert the Magnificent (Robert I). Robert the Magnificent had another mistress, with whom he had a daughter, Adelaide. William was sometimes referred to in derogatory terms as William the Bastard. His mother was later married to Herluin de Conteville.

William's father became a Duke after the sudden death of Richard III, the elder brother of William's father. There was a rumor that William's father killed his brother Richard III. However, the story was never proved.

William's upbringing in these unusual circumstances may have shaped his character in later life. He ascended to the throne as a Duke when his father died while returning from a pilgrimage in Jerusalem.

It is not hard to imagine the challenges that William encountered when he ascended to the throne as Duke when he was only seven years old, with a history of illegitimate birth.

However, he was able to make it through young adulthood, mainly due to the support of the King of France, Henry I, and his uncle Archbishop Robert.

HISTORICAL SNAPSHOTS OF THE GREAT

When his uncle, Archbishop Robert, died in 1037, a fierce power struggle ensued. Several individuals who were trying hard to protect William were killed. This period of chaos lasted for several years. Alan of Brittany died in 1039. Gilbert of Brionne and Turchetil were murdered a few months later. Osbern was killed in 1040. It was a period of death all around the young Duke.

In 1046, some of his opponents tried to kill him. He escaped at night and was given refuge by King Henry I. In the following year, King Henry I, accompanied by William, attacked and conquered Normandy at the Battle of *Val-ès-Dunes*. William was then installed as the leader of Normandy.

Fighting did not stop for the next six or so years, but William was able to hold his own.

An unusual (almost strange) historical fact is that upon rising to power, William issued a decree prohibiting warfare during certain days of the year, according to the so-called Truce of God. It was as if fighting was in people's DNA, and they just had to continue fighting no matter what. Those were strange times.

William was involved in several other skirmishes, primarily to defend his power. He was able to fight back the invading forces successfully.

Historians state that William enjoyed good health for most of his life. He had great stamina too. However, there is no evidence of his education, so he may have grown up illiterate. He was close to the church, seeking advice from the clergy. He also gave generously to the church.

The King of England, Edward the Confessor, did not have children and had at one time made a promise to William, a distant cousin, that William would succeed him as King. However, on January 5, 1066, King Edward, while lying on his death bed in London, appointed Harold, his brother in law, to succeed him as King of England.

When the news of the crowning of Harold as King of England reached William in Normandy, William was much aggrieved, mainly because in 1054, Harold had sworn under oath in church, the Bayeux Cathedral, committing to support William as King in the event of the death of King Edward. Accordingly, William decided to launch an invasion of England to claim the crown. He planned for the battle meticulously.

Using a contingent of 15,000 soldiers, he sailed across the channel. He launched an attack on October 14, 1066, at the coastal town of Hastings. The landing was unexpected, thanks to William's strategic planning.

At that time, Harold was busy fighting the Norwegians who had attacked from the north of England at Stamford Bridge. Harold's army slaughtered all the Norwegian soldiers in the Battle of Stamford Bridge. But little did Harold know that another battle was looming south of England, which his tired soldiers would have to fight.

So, William's landing in Pevensey beach, in the south of England, on September 28, 1066, did not encounter resistance. His troops disembarked there, while his fleet docked at the nearby village of Hastings.

Harold, on the other hand, assembled his troops at the village of Hastings. The battle started at 9:00 am on October 14, 1066. After fierce fighting for several hours, William pulled some tactical maneuvers that disoriented Harold's soldiers, allowing William to wage a ferocious attack that resulted in the death of many English soldiers, many more than those on William's contingent.

More significantly, Harold himself and his two brothers were killed, breaking the morale of their soldiers, as there was no one to offer effective leadership of the army. William eventually won the battle, which was later referred to as the Battle of Hastings.

William then launched a campaign of terror in the English countryside, killing many people and setting whole villages on fire. This campaign of terror ensured that he eliminated all forms of resistance. On December 25, 1066, he marched into London and was crowned King of England at Westminster Abbey. He was the first Norman to rule England.

An amusing anecdote is that William's half-brother, Odor, a bishop, removed his robe and wore an armored suit. As a man of the cloth, he was forbidden to use the sword to shed blood, so he took a club to fight.

The rule of William the Conqueror was exceptional. He completely transformed England. He confiscated land from the lords, added French words into the English language; introduced an efficient governance system; and built close to 495 castles, including the Tower of London. In 1085, he commissioned a detailed census of people, land, and property. The details were recorded in the so-called Domesday Book (or Doomsday Book).

The Domesday Book is available for public viewing at the National Archives in London [23, 24]. The Domesday Book comprises two volumes, 913 pages in total with 2 million Latin words, covering a detailed census of 13,000 places in England and Wales[25]. One observer of the survey stated that "there was no single hide nor a yard of land, nor indeed one ox nor one cow nor one pig which was left out."[26]

William's rule was characterized by constant revolts, which he quelled through murderous terror.

William died in September 1087 after a short illness. He left behind nine children with his wife Matilda of Flanders. Upon his death, Normandy became part of French territory. The

Normans who had moved into England intermarried with the English and eventually became part of English society.

Genghis Khan

IF THERE WAS A MEDAL for the leader who caused the greatest and the most vicious atrocities in this world, then Genghis Khan would earn that accolade hands down. His brutality was legendary.

The exact date of Genghis Khan's birth is not known but is believed to have been between 1163 and 1167. His original name was Temujin.

Genghis Khan's father was a chief, who died from poisoning by people from a rival tribe when Temujin was only nine years old. The tribal leaders deserted Temujin and his family. The family had no friends and lived with great hardship. This hard life considerably hardened Temujin. He grew into a great warrior.

Life in the Mongolian Steppes was vicious. Violence was the order of the day. His first vicious taste of this violence was when the Merkits tribe attacked Temejin's village, burnt it down, and in the process as hijacked Temujin's wife, Borte. This event had an enormous impact on Temujin. He vowed to mete out revenge on the attackers.

Jointly with his brother Jamuka, Temujin went looking for Borte in the northern hills of Mongolia. They conducted a vicious campaign, during which they also rescued Borte, eight months after she had been abducted.

In a strange unfolding of events, Borte gave birth one month after she was rescued. There were doubts about the real father of the child, but this did not deter Temujin. He loved his wife unconditionally and accepted the child as his own. At this time, Temujin was only 20 years old.

Some historians believe that the kidnapping of Borte had incensed Temujin so intensely that it may have been the primary reason for his vicious brutality against his enemies in later years[27].

Later on, a rift grew between Temujin and his brother Jamuka. Jamuka left with his tribesmen to another location. Two years later, Jamuka launched a vicious attack on Temujin and his tribesmen. Many people died. Jamuka captured about 70 of Temujin's generals and subjected them to the cruelest punishment imaginable. The generals were boiled alive in full view of other villagers.

Temujin received the news of the cruelty subjected to his tribesmen. He vowed to mete out revenge and never to allow his soldiers ever to be subjected to such horrendous cruelty again. He developed a team of warriors who he trained to fight as a team, not as individuals. This was the beginning of organized warfare. The army was organized into a proper hierarchy. He made military training compulsory for everyone in the tribe. The hierarchy in the military was based on merit, not ethnicity. He built a mighty army by the standards of the day.

When Temujin was sure that the army was ready, he headed westwards to confront his brother Jamuka. He had built a disciplined force that would rely not only on physical might but psychological warfare. Temujin deployed incredible military strategies and tactics, butchering Jamuka's soldiers in a manner that had never been seen before. Jamuka's army was obliterated. Jamuka fled into the mountains where he hid.

One year later, Jemuka was captured by his own generals and handed over to Temujin. Temujin ordered the generals executed. He then implored Jamuka to rejoin him. Jamuka refused, despite great persuasion by Temujin. Jamuka requested Temujin to grant him a noble death without spilling his blood. The wish was granted. Jamuka was killed by having his back broken on a pile of stones.

In 1206, following the death of Jamuka, Temujin became the overall leader of all tribes in Mongolia. He was granted the title Genghis Khan (Oceanic Ruler of the Universe).

To consolidate his power, he decided to attack the Chinese on the east. This was no mean feat. He assembled an army of 50,000 soldiers and crossed the Gobi Desert to launch his attack in northern China. His army unleashed untold carnage on the Chinese.

He continued on his warpath to Beijing. But he found a city surrounded by a 40ft wall. It was a significant obstacle that was almost insurmountable. Genghis Khan decided to wage a new type of warfare - laying siege in the city's periphery so that supplies could not get into the city. Many people in the city starved to death. Others resorted to cannibalism for survival.

When Genghis Khan was sure that he had considerably weakened the city, he launched a direct attack. After a fierce battle, Genghis Khan captured Beijing. The plunder and other atrocities that followed were horrendous.

After his ferocious escapades, Genghis Khan introduced a legal system in Mongolia. Things calmed down. After some time, he started looking westwards, sending emissaries to deliver messages to different capitals in Persia.

On one unfortunate occasion, the response that Genghis Khan received was the head of his murdered emissary. Genghis Khan became livid. Whoever did it had grossly miscalculated Genghis Khan's temperament. Genghis Khan put together an army to mete out revenge.

The revenge was exceptionally vicious. Genghis Khan's army killed more than a million people and burned down whole villages across Persia. Inaljuk, the local general who was behind the murder of Genghis Khan's emissary, was captured, and molten metal poured into his eyes and ears.[28]

Genghis Khan did not stop there. He ordered his army to continue further westwards into Europe and Russia. He is quoted as having said that:

> *The Greatest happiness is to scatter your enemy, to drive him before you, to see his cities reduced to ashes, to see those who love him shrouded in tears, and to gather into your bosom his wives and daughters.*

One in 200 people alive today (or 8% of Asians) can trace their lineage back to Genghis Khan.

In 1226, while on a mission to China, Genghis Khan fell from a horse and sustained injuries. He died in 1227 and left the Mongol Kingdom under the leadership of his son Kublai Khan.

The Mongol Empire continued expanding into Europe until the death of Kublai Khan in 1294. The Empire subsequently started shrinking, but Genghis Khan had left an indelible mark in the world. It is unlikely that any man will ever visit so much brutality in such a vast region of the world. It is said that the site of his burial was so secret that anyone who was a witness to the site was murdered to keep it a secret.[29]

CHAPTER 8

Music

Music, even in situations of the greatest horror, should never be painful to the ear but should flatter and charm it, and thereby always remain music.
— *Wolfgang Amadeus Mozart*

ONE OF MY CLOSE FRIENDS at Naivasha Boarding School was Muthemba. We joined the school at the same time in 1968, in Standard Five. We were allocated sleeping and residential quarters in the same dormitory. So, during events involving "dorms," Muthemba and I would be on the same team.

The one big difference between Muthemba and me, especially during our first term after joining the school, was that he was from Nairobi, which was more sophisticated than Nakuru town where I hailed from. Indeed, boys from Nairobi were seen as more cultured than boys from other parts of the country, who were the majority.

Muthemba, being a Nairobian, had gained quite a lot of knowledge about Kenyan musicians, as well as musicians from Tanzania and Congo. At that time, music from Congo was trendy in Kenya, and Muthemba happened to be an expert in Congolese music. He had an exercise book in which he had recorded the lyrics of the most famous Congolese songs. Friends would occasionally gather around his bed in the dorm to listen to him singing the Congolese songs. It was incredible. He was passionate about Congolese music. He maintained the passion throughout his three-year stay at Naivasha Boarding School.

When I finished primary school, I assumed that life in high school would continue just as in primary school. However, the reality was that most boys headed to different secondary schools across the country; many of them never to see each other again.

I met Muthemba two times in Nairobi (my father had relocated our family to Nairobi a few months before I finished my primary school education at Naivasha Boarding School). The times that I met Muthemba were uneventful, but I recall vividly his account of how he was learning to play the guitar.

About ten or so years later, after I had finished high school and joined college, I learned from a friend that Muthemba had joined a band called the Kenya Blue Stars as the bass guitarist. I was amazed.

I became interested in the Kenya Blue Stars and never skipped any newspaper article featuring the band.

Over time, Muthemba became quite a prominent member of the band. Whenever I thought about our school days at Naivasha Boarding School, my mind quickly shifted to the moments when Muthemba's passion for music was in full display. He had truly realized his dreams.

I remember thinking that if someone was passionate about something at a young age, their endeavors in pursuit of that passion would ultimately yield success.

I can confidently say that even if Muthemba was working as a musician to earn a living, he was enjoying his vocation every step of the way. Perhaps this is also true of the great musicians who have had a significant impact on the music scene globally, such as Mozart, Ludwig van Beethoven, and John Lennon.

Wolfgang Mozart

WOLFGANG AMADEUS MOZART WAS BORN on January 27, 1756, in Salzburg, Austria. He was born into a family of musicians. His father, Leopold Mozart, was a music teacher, composer, and violinist. Leopold published a very successful violin textbook.

Mozart was the last born in the family of seven children, five of whom died. Mozart watched closely as his father taught his sister Nannerl how to play the keyboard.

Young Mozart was recognized as a genius in music at an early age. It is said that he wrote his music compositions when he was just six years old. This was exceptional talent by any standard.

Leopold Mozart taught his children music, languages, and other subjects. There is no historical record of any other type of education that Mozart received. Still, his father was entirely devoted to what he was teaching his two children.

In 1762 the family traveled extensively in Munich, Prague, and Vienna, during which Young Nannerl and Mozart performed for the nobility. That was not all. They went as far as Paris, London, Dover, the Hague, Amsterdam, Utrecht, and Mechelen, during which the two children performed to different audiences.

The trips were challenging and caused great hardship for the family. The tours were long, and travel was by a carriage, which made the trips quite tiring. Sometimes the children fell ill. And payments for performances were sometimes delayed.

In 1769, Leopold went on another trip to Italy, this time with only the 14-year-old Mozart, leaving Nannerl and her mother at home. The tours were very successful.

One year after completing the Italy trip, Mozart gained full-time employment as a court musician in Salzburg. After a short time, he moved to Vienna, where his music career blossomed. He composed sonatas (music played on a single piano or piano accompanied by a violin), concertos (one-star performer playing one instrument with background music played by an orchestra), and symphonies (where the orchestra is the center of attraction); and operas (where musicians sing a "story" on stage).

By the time of his death on December 5, 1791, at the young age of 35, he had more than 600 music compositions to his credit.

My favorite Mozart tune is No. 9 Symphony No. 40 in G minor, K. 550, which I am willing to bet has been heard by almost everybody within [+ or -10] years my age. Other popular tunes are No. 8 Piano Concerto No. 21 in C major and No.2 Turkish March. I also enjoy No. 1 – Eine Klein Nachtmusik K.525, Sonata No. 16 KV 545, and Rondo Alla Turka.

Ludwig Beethoven

LUDWIG VAN BEETHOVEN WAS BORN on December 16, 1770, in Bonn, Germany. He grew into a classical musical genius despite an unusually harsh upbringing.

Beethoven's father, Johann van Beethoven, was a Flemish-German musician, teacher, and singer. Beethoven's grandfather, Ludwig van Beethoven (1712–1773), was also a musician.

Beethoven's father was a strict disciplinarian and forced Beethoven to learn music the hard way. When Beethoven failed to follow his father's instructions, he was severely beaten. At one time, when his mother tried to intervene, she too was beaten, an event that greatly disturbed Beethoven. He swore to perform better in his music, not because of his love for it, but as a way of preventing his mother from getting further beatings from his father.

Beethoven also received coaching from the organist Gilles van den Eeden, keyboard lessons from a family friend named Tobias Friedrich Pfeiffer, and violin and viola lessons from a relative named Franz Rovantini. The training started when Beethoven was only five years old. It was intensive training. Sometimes he would be woken up late at night to practice on the keyboard.

When Beethoven was 21, he was noticed by Count Ferdinand Ernst Gabriel von Waldstein. The Count sponsored him to travel to Vienna, where he was exposed to other accomplished musicians such as Mozart.

While in Vienna, Beethoven met Joseph Haydn, who taught him a lot about music. Interestingly, Beethoven did not play his music in paid concerts. He relied on donations that were not always forthcoming.

Beethoven's father slid into alcoholism, forcing Beethoven to take responsibility for maintaining his two siblings.

Beethoven lived quite an unconventional lifestyle. He was untidy and mingled with people in unexpected social circles, despite his prominence as a good musician. He used to say: "There are and always will be thousands of princes, but there is only one Beethoven!"

In another unfortunate turn of events, Beethoven started developing deafness when he was in his twenties. In 1811, he became completely deaf. But amazingly, he continued to compose great music despite the deafness.

Some of Beethoven's greatest tunes include Sonata in C sharp minor, op. 27, nr. 2 "The Moonlight Sonata," Symphony No. 5 in C minor, and Symphony No. 9 in D minor, "Ode to Joy."

Beethoven died on March 26, 1827. More than 10,000 people witnessed his funeral. He was indeed one of the greatest pianists and composers. His compositions were innovative, combining vocals and instruments in new ways. He is credited with the composition of nine symphonies, five piano concertos, one violin concerto, 32 piano sonatas, 16 string quartets, two masses, and the opera Fidelio.

John Lennon

JOHN LENNON WAS BORN IN LIVERPOOL in October 1940. His story is probably one of the most unusual of individuals who grew into significant figures on the world music stage.

John Lennon's father, Alfred Lennon, was an Irish seaman who spent a lot of time away from home. He was absent during John Lennon's birth. John Lennon, therefore, spent most of his time under the care of his mother.

Alfred's long absences had unfortunate consequences. His wife, Julia (John Lennon's mother), became pregnant with another man. And when Alfred returned to Liverpool, Julia did not accept him.

Julia's elder sister Mimi took custody of John Lennon. In 1946, in an unusual twist of events, Alfred took Lennon away from Mimi. The news reached Julia. She confronted Alfred, intending to take John Lennon back from him. It was an ugly incident during which the young John Lennon was asked to choose between his father or his mother. John Lennon decided to go with his mother.

John Lennon spent the rest of his childhood in Woolton, under the care of Mimi and her husband, George Toogood Smith. The couple willingly accepted the responsibility as they did not have a child of their own. Julia visited John Lennon regularly.

John Lennon's interest in music may have been triggered by his uncle, who bought him a mouth organ. Also, when John was around 11 years old, he used to visit his mother at Liverpool, where she would play for him Elvis Presley records. She also taught him how to play the banjo.

John spent a lot of his time with his cousin Stanley Parkes and other friends. So, despite the exceptional parental circumstances, he did have an opportunity to socialize well with his agemates.

After leaving primary school, John joined Quarry Bank High School in Liverpool. He stayed there from 1952 to 1957. He was said to be a "happy-go-lucky, good-humored, easy going, lively lad."

John received his first guitar in 1956 from his mother, Julia. He lost his mother in 1958 when she died from a car accident.

Lennon was a highly mischievous student in high school. His incessant misbehavior was mirrored in his final "O" level grades. He failed in all subjects. However, following the intervention of his aunt, he was admitted to the Liverpool College of Art. He was thrown out of the college in the final year due to misbehavior.

But John was an unusual youngster. In September 1956, when he was 15, he formed the Quarrymen band. Paul

McCartney joined the band later. George Harrison, then only 14 years old, also joined the band as the lead guitarist, while Stuart Sutcliffe joined as the bass guitarist. The four individuals formed the Beatles in 1960. Pete Best joined a little later as the drummer.

The band got contracts in Germany that kept them busy for the following two years. The band hired Brian Epstein as their manager. He played this role for several years until his demise in 1967.

After the gigs in Germany, Stuart Sutcliffe decided to remain in Germany. Paul McCartney took over as the bass guitarist. The drummer, Pete Best, too, was replaced by Ringo Star. The remaining quartet of musicians took the Beatles to unparalleled heights in the music industry globally.

The Beatles broke up in 1969. John Lennon decided to pursue a solo career. He sold more than 14 million records. By the end of 2019, the Beatles, as a group, had sold the highest number of records in recorded history with more than 600 million albums to their credit.[3031]

John Lennon's life as a solo musician was full of intrigue. He dabbled in political activism, which was bruising. He died on December 8, 1980, in New York from a gunshot fired by one of his fans, David Chapman.

CHAPTER 9

Philosophy

The philosophers have only interpreted the world in various ways. The point, however, is to change it.
—*Karl Marx*

I HAVE OFTEN WONDERED WHY philosophy is not taught in primary and high schools in Kenya, considering the number and intricacy of philosophical questions that many students grapple with as they go through primary and high school. Even children who have not reached school-going age sometimes ask questions of such deep philosophical significance that parents sometimes have difficulty answering the questions.

One of our favorite pass times during week-ends when I was at Naivasha Boarding School was to sit next to a wall facing the Naivasha-Nakuru highway whilst soaking up the sun. The wall could only accommodate about twenty students.

So, immediately after breakfast, students would rush from the dining hall like mad to secure a spot on the wall.

If one was lucky to stake a claim to a spot on the wall, then they would be assured of several hours of exciting stories. The typical sequence of subjects covered was (1) teachers, (2) other students, (3) politics, and (4) girls. Topic (4) would consume the most significant amount of time, as there were many experts on the subject.

On a few occasions, and depending upon who was in the group, students would end up getting into deep philosophical questions.

What is Philosophy?

PERHAPS THE BEST STARTING POINT of finding out what philosophy means is to look at the definition in the Simple English Wikipedia:

> *Philosophy is a way of thinking about the world, the universe, and society. It works by asking very basic questions about the nature of human thought, the nature of the universe, and the connections between them. The ideas in philosophy are often general and abstract. But this does not mean that philosophy is not about the real world. Ethics, for example, asks about how to be good in our day-to-day lives. Metaphysics asks about how the world works and what it is made of.[32]*

I like this definition for its simplicity. Over time, philosophical questions have been grouped into several distinct branches. We will look at the main branches briefly. But if philosophy is not your thing, please do not be put off by the high-sounding terminology.

Firstly, we have a branch of philosophy called metaphysics. This branch of philosophy deals with reality. So, when you ask questions about the existence of things or how things in existence relate to each other, then you are asking metaphysical questions. Metaphysics is divided into different categories, but we will not get into that here.

Secondly, we have epistemology. This is the branch of philosophy that deals with questions of knowledge. In other words, what is knowledge, and how do we acquire it? Are we born with certain types of knowledge inherent in our minds, or do we acquire knowledge through learning? Or, more fundamentally, how do we justify knowledge claims?

Thirdly, we have an exciting branch of philosophy called ethics, which deals with questions of right and wrong. In other words, questions of morality. For example, when you ask whether it is right or wrong for someone to kill someone else in self-defense, you are asking a question related to the branch of philosophy called ethics. If someone walked into a room brandishing a gun and said that he was looking for your friend

Mr. X, would it be right or wrong for you to be truthful about Mr. X's whereabouts? This is an example of an ethical question.

Ethical questions are some of the most interesting in philosophy. Indeed, when we sat at the wall at Naivasha Boarding School, ethical issues were the most common philosophical questions that would emerge from time to time.

Fourthly, we have the branch of philosophy called aesthetics, which deals with questions of beauty. For example, what is it that makes a work of art beautiful?

Fifthly, we have logic. This is the branch of philosophy that deals with correct reasoning. A few popular syllogisms are used to illustrate the use of logical reasoning. One famous one was by Socrates, which went as follows: "All men are mortal. Socrates is a man. Therefore, I am mortal." It is possible to see defects in reasoning using rules of logic.

Consider the following syllogism: "All crows are black. The bird in my cage is black. Therefore, this bird is a crow." It should be evident that the conclusion drawn from the premises of this statement is false. It is a fallacy. By applying the rules of logic, it is possible to detect such errors in reasoning.

Several individuals are credited with making valuable contributions to the field of philosophy. They include Lao Tzu (c. 601 -531 BC), the founder of Taoism, Confucius (c. 551-479 BC) who is renowned for his wisdom on morality, and Socrates (c. 469-399 BC), the Greek philosopher who is said to be the father of western philosophy, and who famously said: "The unexamined life is not worth living."

Other philosophers include Plato (c. 423 BC – 348 BC), who was a student of Socrates and who is credited for having started the Academy, the first institution of higher learning in the western world; and Aristotle (c. 384BC – 322BC), a polymath who made significant contributions not only in philosophy but in other fields too. Aristotle is one of my favorite ancient scholars.

Other notable philosophers who made significant contributions are Rene Descartes (1596 – 1650), a French philosopher who is famous for his profoundly philosophical statement: "I think; therefore, I am.", John Locke (1632-1704), an English philosopher renowned for his philosophical ideas on politics, and Voltaire (1694 – 1778), a French philosopher whose satirical ideas helped trigger the French Revolution.

Other great historical figures in philosophy include Jean Jacques Rousseau (1712-1778), also a French philosopher whose writings also helped to spur the French Revolution; Adam Smith (1723-1790), a social philosopher from Scotland and great classical economist; and Karl Marx (1818-1883), a German philosopher who founded Marxism which had a profound impact on world politics. Also, Jean-Paul Sartre (1905-1980), a French philosopher who wrote prolifically and is credited with developing ideas on existentialism.

In the interest of brevity, we will explore the lives of three of these philosophers, namely, Aristotle, Jean Jacques Rousseau, and Karl Marx.

Aristotle

WHEN I FIRST READ the history of Aristotle, I was utterly mesmerized by his numerous contributions in philosophy and many other fields.

Aristotle was born in Stagira, Greece, around 384 BC. He lost his parents when he was 13 years old. He was raised by a guardian called Proxenus of Atarneus, his older sister's husband.

Aristotle joined Plato's Academy in Athens when he was about 18 years old. The main subjects taught at the academy were philosophy, mathematics, and astronomy. The Academy encouraged students to ponder over problems and to find solutions. Students were encouraged to engage in discussion rather than merely listening to lectures. The idea was to encourage students to reach solutions through well-reasoned arguments. His education at the Plato Academy lasted about 20 years, after which he left for Lesbos.

Aristotle married Pythias while at Lesbos. Pythias gave birth to a daughter.

During his time at Lesbos, Aristotle conducted detailed research in botany and zoology. His research findings were exceptionally detailed, capturing minute details of more than 500 species, and lay the foundations of a new scientific discipline, biology.

In 343 BC, at the invitation of King Philip II, Aristotle traveled to Macedonia to head the Royal Academy of Macedon and to tutor King Philip's son, Alexander.

In 355 BC, Aristotle established his academy in Athens, the Lyceum. He taught at the academy for 12 years, during which he produced some of his greatest works. He wrote various treatises, notably, *Physics, Metaphysics, and Nicomachean Ethics; Politics, On the Soul, and Poetics*. He made significant and wide-ranging contributions in logic, metaphysics, and mathematics; physics, biology, and botany; ethics, politics, and agriculture; medicine, dance, and theatre. He laid the foundations of western intellectual thought.

Aristotle died in 322 BC at the age of 62, while on the island of Euboea, where he had fled to escape persecution by the rulers in Athens who accused him of blasphemy. The same accusation had been leveled against Socrates several years earlier.

Jean Jacques Rousseau

JEAN JACQUES ROUSSEAU IS AN example of the enormous impact that one person's written words can have on society. His satirical writings helped trigger the French Revolution.[33]

Jean Jacques Rousseau was born on June 28, 1712, in Geneva. His mother died nine days later due to a fever. His father, Isaac Rousseau, was a clock-maker.

Rousseau's father left Geneva due to political pressure. He left Rousseau, who was ten years old at the time, under the care of relatives.

Rousseau did not get much formal education. He became an apprentice to a notary and engraver, but things did not work out well for him. He left for Savoy to look for greener pastures. While in Savoy, he fell in love with a 29-year old lady, Françoise-Louise de Warens, an outgoing character. De Warens was a great entertainer, loved music and literature, and was also a spendthrift.

Through the support of de Warens, Rousseau learned philosophy, music, mathematics, and other subjects.

Rousseau moved to Paris in 1742. In 1745, he fell in love with a laundry maid called Thérèse Levasseur, and they got married.

While in Paris, he became friends with Denis Diderot. He collaborated with Diderot in the publication of a radical, anti-ecclesiastical magazine called *Encyclopaedia*. Rousseau's writings in the magazine stood out as the most influential. His friend Diderot was imprisoned for anti-ecclesiastical writings in the magazine. This event evoked strong emotions in Rousseau, who decided to pursue a more radical line in his writings. He became a prominent critic of tradition, both in philosophy and in music, in which he was well versed. His books started gaining wide recognition.

In 1761, he published a novel entitled *Julie*, whose underlying message was how to reject social norms. The book was a major success, turning Rousseau into a celebrity.

The *Social Contract* followed in 1762. It was an immensely influential political work in which Rousseau advocated for the liberty of man. A new social contract where all members of society were equal.

Emile followed the *Social Contract*, also in 1762, in which Rousseau talked at length about the correct type of education for children – education free of the corrupting influences of society. The book also presented the view that belief in God was universal, irrespective of religious affiliation. This suggested that all religions were equal, invoking the wrath of those in authority. In 1762, *Emile* was banned in Geneva and Paris.

Rousseau fled to Switzerland, but he was not welcome there either. He subsequently relocated to Prussia, which was under Frederick the Great. His visit there did not last long. The local community there did not like him because of his writings, which they considered blasphemous. At some point, they even pelted him with stones. He moved back to Switzerland after two years. But he was still not welcome there. Eventually, he moved to England at the invitation of the philosopher David Hume.

His relationship with Hume did not last long, owing to negative sentiments in the community due to Rousseau's writing, which had started appearing in the local press. He returned to France in 1767 under a false name to avoid arrest.

In 1776, Rousseau was knocked down by a dog in a Paris Street. He sustained injuries that led to his death two years later.

The French Revolution occurred ten years after Rousseau's death. The people behind the revolution used Rousseau's ideas on egalitarianism as their guiding philosophy. Some historians believe that Rousseau's ideas also played a part in the American Revolution of 1765 – 1783.

Karl Marx

WHEN I WAS IN HIGH SCHOOL, there was a popular joke that following students' unrest at the University of Nairobi, the President of the country had issued orders for the arrest of Karl Marx, whom he had been told was primarily responsible for triggering the disturbance. That joke perhaps illustrates the significant influence that Karl Marx has had on society in general. There is an engraving on his tomb which reads: "The philosophers have only interpreted the world, in various ways. The point, however, is to change it." One could not have thought of a better message to capture the essence of Karl Mar's philosophy.

Some believe that Karl Marx's influence on the world order was positive. Others have an opposite view: that his philosophy was evil and caused immense suffering in many parts of the world. The fact that people have held such diametrically different views on Karl Mark's philosophy just goes to show the magnitude of his persona as an enigma.

Karl Marx was born on May 5, 1818, in Trier, Germany, the third born in a family of nine children. He was baptized in the Lutheran Church in 1824. His father, Heinrich Marx, was a lawyer who was originally a follower of Judaism but changed to Christianity. Karl Marx's mother, Henriette Pressburg, was the daughter of a wealthy Jewish textile merchant from the Netherlands. Her family founded the Phillips Electronics Company.

Karl Marx's father was a political radical, involved in the agitation for constitutional reforms in Prussia, then under the rule of the monarchy.

Karl Marx received private tuition from his father until 1830, when he was about 12 years old. He then joined Trier High School. Many of the teachers in the school championed doctrines of political liberalism and distributed literature along these lines to students. (The fundamental idea of liberalism is the enhancement of individual freedom.) When the authorities learned about what was happening in the school, they replaced some of the teachers.

Karl Marx joined the University of Bonn in October 1835 when he was 17 years old. He enrolled for a degree in law at the insistence of his father.

It would appear that he followed his father's footsteps, including becoming a radical. He joined the Poets' Club, a club of radicals who were under constant surveillance by the government. He also joined and even became co-president of the Trier Tavern Club drinking society. In August 1836, he participated in a duel with a member of the Borussia Korps.

Karl Marx became a problem student. His grades started deteriorating. In an attempt to salvage the situation, his father transferred him to the University of Berlin.

His move to the University of Berlin was a good turning point in his academic performance. He became more serious.

In 1836, he was involved in a controversial romantic relationship with Jenny von Westphalen, baroness of the Prussian ruling class. He married her seven years later.

When he joined the University of Berlin, he developed a keen interest in philosophy. However, his primary degree program was in law. He became very interested in the philosophy of Friedrich Hegel. He joined the students' Doctor's Club, which advocated the philosophical ideas of Hegel. He also joined the Young Hegelians in 1837, a group of student radicals.

In 1837, Marx wrote some short fictional and non-fictional novels. He also wrote some poems. He stopped writing the novels so that he could study English, Italian, art history, and the translation of Latin classics.

Marx's father died in 1838, leaving a big void in Marx's life.

Marx wrote his doctoral thesis in 1841, which was acclaimed as a powerful piece of work. "A daring and original piece of work in which Marx set out to show that theology must yield to the superior wisdom of philosophy." [34] He submitted his thesis to the University of Jena, where he was awarded a Ph.D. in April 1841.

In July 1841, Marx and his friend Bauer traveled to Bonn. They got drunk and were seen laughing in church and misbehaving on the streets of Bonn.

In 1842, Marx moved to Cologne. He joined the radical newspaper *Rheinische Zeitung* (Rhineland News) as a journalist. The government later banned the paper for publishing subversive material.

In 1843, Marx moved to Paris and joined another radical newspaper, the *Deutsch-Französische Jahrbücher* (German-French Annals), as a co-editor. The paper was banned in the German states after only one issue. Marx then joined *Vorwärts!* (Forward!), where he wrote socialist-leaning articles.

In August 1844, Marx met Friedrich Engels. They became great friends, collaborating on several writing projects. Engels convinced Marx that the working class would bring about the final revolution in history. One of Marx's early controversial philosophical works was a book entitled *Communism Economic and Philosophical Manuscripts of 1844*.

During the three years that Marx lived in Paris, he studied political economy intensely, and French history, and the French socialists.

In 1845, *Vorwärts!* was banned by the French government, and Marx was expelled from the country. He moved to

Brussels in February 1845. His friend Engels followed him there in April of the same year. In July 1845, both gentlemen left for England.

While in England, Marx and Engels wrote extensively on their socialistic ideas. However, the work that was later to have the most significant impact on society was a pamphlet entitled *Communist Manifesto,* which was first published in February 1848.

The primary purpose of the *Communist Manifesto* was to communicate to the public the aims and objectives of the Communist League. It articulated how society had been characterized by class struggles and the attendant antagonism between the wealthy owners of capital, the bourgeoisie, and the working class, the proletariat. The *Manifesto* further outlined how the Communist League was best suited to bring down the exploitative bourgeoisie and replace it with a more equitable and just socialist system.

Shortly after the publication of the Communist Manifesto, civil unrest emerged in different parts of Europe, including a revolution in France. Karl Marx actively supported the civil unrest, using funds that had been bequeathed to him by his father, previously withheld by his uncle Philips after Karl Marx's father's death in 1838.

Karl Marx spent the rest of his life in England. His major preoccupation was researching and writing. His writing was mainly focused on political economy and how to influence society to take action to correct what he perceived as an unjust economic system. His most influential work in political economy was *Das Capital*, a 1,134-page volume, published in 1867[35]. *Das Capital* was mainly a critique of the capitalist system and promoted socialism as the ultimate substitute for capitalism.

The central argument of *Das Capital* was that the productive system in an economy was comprised of three key elements, the so-called "trinity formula" for redistribution of surplus-value in an enterprise: (1) the landowners who get rent, (2) the workers who get wages, and (3) the providers of capital who get profits.[36]

Marx argued that in the ideal system, the net output would be shared equitably between the three players based on their respective contributions to the enterprise. However, in the capitalist system, what happened was that the aggregate surplus-value of an enterprise (in essence, the unpaid wages) ends up in the pockets of the capitalists at different levels of the ruling class. In other words, industrial production in a capitalist system is founded on the exploitation of the workers.[37]

My simple interpretation of the basic tenets of his philosophy was as follows: he believed that society had evolved to create a capitalist system where a few individuals became owners of the means of production (the bourgeoisie), and the majority became the workers (the proletariat). Further, he believed that the capitalist system was skewed unjustly in favor of the bourgeoisie, who exploited the proletariat in their capitalist production system. Also, this unjust system needed to be changed so that everyone could be equal. However, because the bourgeoisie was so entrenched in the capitalist system, the only feasible way of bringing about change was by force, through a revolution by the proletariat. So, he spent a considerable amount of time persuading the working class to recognize the chains that had been put on them by the bourgeoisie and to unite so that they could free themselves from the shackles of exploitation by the bourgeoisie. This, in my view, was the essence of Marxist philosophy.

He did not achieve the kind of success that he was looking for in triggering a worldwide revolution. However, years after his death, many individuals used his name and ideas to cause untold death and destruction in different parts of the world. The best examples are Joseph Stalin in Russia and Mao Ze Dong in China. Several other regimes across the globe toyed with Marxist ideas, but the majority ended up with disastrous results.

Karl Marx died in London, England, on March 14, 1883, at 64, after an extended illness.

CHAPTER 10

Politics

M Y FIRST ENCOUNTER WITH RAW political power happened in the first term of school in 1969 at Naivasha Boarding School. Traditionally, the first significant business of the school during the first one or two weeks of a new school year was the appointment of school prefects and a Bell Ringer. These were powerful positions. Prefects had tremendous sway over the affairs of students.

Prefects enjoyed various other privileges. For example, they enjoyed the comfort of a bed at the end of the dormitory, next to the wall. Also, a prefect's bed was placed at a comfortable distance from the other beds for maximum unfettered comfort of this important individual. During the few times when meat was included in lunch or dinner, prefects received several nice lumpy chunks each, while lesser mortals received only one small piece each.

Additionally, when the meal included *ugali* (a thick paste of pounded maizemeal), which was 99.9% of the time, prefects ate the hard and delicious crust (*mukuro*) found at the bottom of the cooking pot. And since the prefects could not finish all the available *mukuro*, a few other lucky students got a chance to enjoy it too.

But luck in this context was like winning a lottery. You had to be at the ideal spot on the lunch queue to pick a plate of ugali containing *mukuro*. So, before joining the queue, you had to carefully cast your eyes across the tens of plates on the lunch table and make the best estimate possible of where to join the line so that you would arrive at the lunch table at precisely the right moment to pick the plate containing *mukuro*. It was an exercise in advanced heuristics.

The opportunity of eating *mukuro* every day was the most significant privilege bestowed upon prefects. Many students, therefore, aspired to be appointed prefects.

The Bell Ringer, on the other hand, while an important individual in the student community and regarded with respect, did not enjoy the privileges of the prefects. It was one of those thankless roles with tremendous responsibility but no accompanying perks.

The Bell Ringer had to wake up early to ring the bell to wake up other students. He also had to ring the bell to prompt students to go for the morning parade.

That was not all. He also had to ring the bell at the end of morning lessons, at the beginning of afternoon lessons, and at the end of the day after the last lesson. It was an important position that boosted the profile of the individual assigned to it. Perhaps a good item on the student's CV.

However, something unusual happened in January 1969. The teachers "forgot" to appoint prefects and the Bell Ringer within the normal one to two-week period. We never got to know the underlying reason for this omission. However, I can vividly recall how some students, almost from the blue, decided to nominate themselves as prefects. These individuals included Karanja (not his real name), who was always last in class in academic performance. He had no chance in hell of becoming a prefect. Still, he managed to secure a corner bed in the dormitory for himself, the privilege of enjoying *mukuro* during meal times, ordering other children around, and meting out punishment willy nilly like a "real prefect," thanks to his brute force. It was raw political dictatorship at its core.

The small community of school children had spontaneously mutated into a society of the rulers and the ruled. The "rulers" were exceptionally ruthless to the other students (the "ruled"). Strangely enough, students did not seem to have any say in the matter. They just acquiesced to the status quo like sheep in a herd. Teachers probably became aware of what was happening, but my sense at the time was that they did not care less.

The teachers appointed an official student leadership body well into the second month of the term. This brought some sanity to the school's leadership hierarchy. Ignorami such as Karanja, and other uncouth individuals, were not appointed as prefects, to the immense joy of those who had suffered under their dictatorship.

Strangely, some of those who had usurped power illegally were appointed prefects and continued to exercise their powers for the remainder of the year.

The situation at Naivasha Boarding School in January 1969 was exceptionally bizarre. It was reminiscent of some political dictatorship systems that exist in the world today. However, from that system emerged a few individuals who seemed to have leadership qualities ingrained in their DNA, who were nominated to do what they were already good at.

This chapter will explore three politicians in history who have had a significant impact on world politics, either positively or negatively. The individuals represent my personal biases, based on what I believe were the individuals' unique attributes. In other words, the individuals from whom we can learn something of value in terms of bettering our individual or collective futures.

The three individuals are Abraham Lincoln (1809-1865), the American President who helped end the scourge of slavery; Adolf Hitler (1889 – 1945), one of the cruelest dictators who ever walked on the world stage; and Mikhail Gorbachev, who presided over the collapse of the former Soviet Union and the opening up of popular democracy in the eastern countries.

Abraham Lincoln

ABRAHAM LINCOLN WAS BORN IN Kentucky on February 12, 1809. He was the second born in the family of Thomas Lincoln and Nancy Hanks Lincoln. His parents belonged to the Baptist Church, where alcohol consumption, dancing, and owning slaves were forbidden. Lincoln's father was a cabinetmaker and carpenter.

In 1816, when Abraham Lincoln was seven years old, the Lincoln family moved to Indiana.

The Thomas Lincoln family lived through a lot of hardship throughout the period when Abraham was a young boy. In 1818, when Abraham Lincoln was nine years old, his mother died. His 11-year old sister, Sarah Lincoln Grigsby, was left with the burden of taking care of the family of four (including Thomas Lincoln). In 1819, Thomas Lincoln married Sarah Bush Johnston, who had three children of her own. Abraham Lincoln developed a very close relationship with his new foster mother, Sarah.

Abraham Lincoln hated farm labor. It is possible that this dislike of farm labor was a result of the harsh treatment that he often received from his father. There are times when his father beat him. Some historians believe that this cruel treatment by his father led Abraham Lincoln to despise slavery.

As a teenager, Abraham Lincoln did various odd jobs outside his father's farm, mainly splitting logs and other types of manual labor. He handed all his earnings to his father. He continued doing this until age 21.

The family of Thomas Lincoln moved to Illinois in 1830. In 1831, Abraham Lincoln, who by then had grown distant from his father, left the family home and moved to New Salem in Menard County, Illinois.

Abraham Lincoln loved education greatly. He was a voracious reader, a habit that he retained for most of his life. He did not receive much formal education, though. Most of his training was through self-study. And through hard work, he passed his law examinations in April 1837, when he was 28 years old. Shortly after that, he received a practicing license.

He worked as a lawyer in Illinois courts. He gained an excellent reputation as an ambitious, driven, and hard-working individual. He had a great sense of humor and was optimistic about human nature. He also had a knack for effectively handling challenging situations and often encouraged people to resolve disputes amicably instead of going to court. He was also an excellent orator as a lawyer and a quick thinker on his feet.

In 1842, Abraham Lincoln married Mary Todd Lincoln, the daughter of a wealthy slave owner in Kentucky. They bore four children. Three of the children died in later years—Edward Baker Lincoln in 1850, William Wallace Lincoln in 1862, and Tad Lincoln in 1871. The deaths of these three sons caused tremendous heartache to Abraham Lincoln and his wife.

Abraham Lincoln developed an interest in public office and, in 1847, stood for elections. He was elected to the House of Representatives for Illinois. He gradually grew in stature as a politician. He went through the typical political ups and downs, including losing elections for a senatorial seat in 1858.

He gained excellent recognition in the Republican Party. In 1860, he was nominated the Republican Presidential candidate.

He successfully contested the elections to become the 16th President of the United States of America in 1861.

Abraham Lincoln became President at an exceptionally challenging time in US history. Even before he was sworn into office, seven states decided to secede from the United States of America. These states were South Carolina, Florida, Mississippi, Alabama, Georgia, Louisiana, and Texas. Six of these states declared themselves sovereign, the Confederate States of America, with an independent constitution, with Jefferson Davis as interim President. Lincoln termed the secession illegal and did not recognize it.

There was tremendous tension in the country triggered primarily by opposing sentiments about the practice of slavery. The southern states wanted slavery extended and detested Abraham Lincoln's ascension to power because he was anti-slavery. He even received assassination threats and had to travel in disguise during part of his journey to Washington for his inauguration on March 4, 1861.

The American Civil War started about a month after Lincoln's inauguration. The war was triggered by an attack on April 12, 1861, by the Confederate forces at Fort Sumter, South Carolina.

The war continued unabated for four years until the surrender of the Confederate army led by Robert E. Lee to

Ulysses S. Grant at Appomattox Courthouse on April 9, 1865. Approximately 620,000 people died during the Civil War.

During his tenure as President, Abraham Lincoln drafted legislation to outlaw slavery in the United States of America, giving hope to millions of black Americans.

Lincoln was re-elected President in 1864. Unfortunately, he did not discharge his duties as President for long. John Wilkes Booth assassinated him on Good Friday, April 14, 1865.

Abraham Lincoln left a commendable legacy as the man who eliminated slavery in the USA and held the Union together despite enormous challenges.

Adolf Hitler

APART FROM GENGHIS KHAN, I cannot think of another human being who caused havoc on as wide a scale as Adolf Hitler. He was responsible for the killing of six million Jews in gas chambers. He was mostly responsible for the onset of the Second World War, during which more than 70 million people died. And this happened less than 100 years ago. Adolf Hitler was a strange human being indeed.

Adolf Hitler was born in Austria in 1889 in a family of modest means. He was the fourth born in a family of six children. Three of his siblings died as infants. His father, Alois Hitler, moved the family to Passau in Germany when Adolf

Hitler was three years old. The family returned to Austria in 1894, when Hitler was five years old.

Adolf Hitler grew up as a loner and did not show much promise academically. He often got into conflict with his father, who occasionally beat him. At some point, Adolf Hitler became a member of the church choir. He even harbored ideas of becoming a priest.

He did not finish secondary school. In 1907, he tried to get into Art school in Vienna two times but was rejected. His mother died in December of the same year.

He struggled immensely while in Vienna. He worked as a casual laborer and also made a little money from the sale of watercolor paintings. At some point, he even ran out of money and had to live in homeless shelters. He moved to Munich, Germany, in 1913 when he was around 24 years old.

Adolf Hitler joined the German army in August 1914, just as the First World War was beginning. He rose to the rank of Corporal. He participated in the First Battle of Ypres, the Battle of the Somme, the Battle of Arras, and the Battle of Passchendaele. He received three awards for bravery, the Iron Cross, Second Class in 1914, the Iron Cross First Class in August 1918, and the Black Wound Badge in May 1918.

Adolf Hitler was extremely bitter about the humiliating German surrender and the stiff penalties imposed on Germany in the Treaty of Versailles at the end of the war.

Adolf Hitler joined the Nazi party, the National Socialist German Workers Party (NSDAP) in 1919. He was member number 555. It is noteworthy that the numbering started at 500 to give the impression of large party membership. He became a full-time worker in the party in April 1920.

Adolf Hitler became an extremely vocal member of the party and a skilled political schemer and manipulator. He gained popularity for his controversial vitriolic rhetoric that criticized the Treaty of Versailles, other politicians, and Marxists, and Jews.

He became an exceptional demagogue. He had a hypnotic effect on audiences. One writer stated that in a 1936 parade, some members of the audience were so entranced by his oratory that they experienced hysteria.[38]

On November 8, 1923, when Hitler was 34, capitalizing on the disillusionment of people in Germany due to an economic slump, Hitler led a *coup de etat*, known as the "Beer Hall Putsch," against the government of Germany. The police foiled the coup. Hitler was captured from hiding after two days and tried in court for high treason.

He was imprisoned for five years but served only nine months after a pardon by the Bavarian Supreme Court. During his time in prison, he wrote the highly controversial political manifesto *Mein Kampf* ("*My Struggle*"), in which he articulated his anti-semitic ideology. The book was initially entitled *Four and a Half Years of Struggle against Lies, Stupidity, and Cowardice.*

When he came out of prison in 1924, Hitler jumped straight back into politics, rising quickly in rank within the party. His popularity was primarily due to his oratory skills and his anti-Semitic and anti-communist propaganda. He won elections in 1933, becoming the Chancellor of Germany in 1934 and President in the same year after the death of Hindenburg. His book, *Mein Kampf,* sold a million copies during his first year in office in 1933.

Adolf Hitler immediately started a program of economic transformation in Germany and achieved great success. As he was doing this, he targeted the Jewish population, which he said was responsible for most of Germany's economic ills. He established the secret police, the Gestapo, who did his bidding. He relentlessly went after his perceived enemies, particularly the Jews.

After consolidating his political position, he started looking outwards to conquer other nations in Europe to expand his "empire." His expansionist program started gaining some traction. He annexed Austria and the Sudetenland part of Czechoslovakia. And in 1938, he annexed the entire nation of Czechoslovakia.

When he invaded Poland in September 1939, the French and British governments decided not to sit idly by watching the

Hitler menace unfolding in Europe. They knew that if they did not act decisively, they would be next in the Hitler expansionist agenda. Accordingly, France and Britain declared war on Germany. That was the beginning of World War II. And even while this was going on, in June 1941, Hitler decided to attack the Soviet Union too. Meanwhile, the Americans decided to join the war on the side of France and Britain.

In 1944, Hitler noticed that he was about to suffer a humiliating defeat and committed suicide.

Mikhail Gorbachev

MIKHAIL GORBACHEV PLAYED A SIGNIFICANT role in bringing the cold war to a close and laying the foundations for democracy in the former Soviet Union and eastern European countries. He received the Nobel Peace Prize in 1990 in recognition of the significant role he played in facilitating a more peaceful world than he found when he rose to power in the Soviet Union.

Mikhail Sergeyevich Gorbachev was born in Privolnoye, Stavropol Krai, to a poor peasant family in the former Soviet

Union. In 1934, when he was three years old, he moved to live with his maternal grandparents in a kolkhoz (collective farm).

The 1930s were difficult times in the Soviet Union. Joseph Stalin was in power and had unleashed untold misery on citizens of the Soviet Union with his massive rural collectivization initiative. For example, between 1936 and 1938, during The Great Purge, people who were seen not to subscribe to Stalin's Communist ideology were rounded up and imprisoned in labor camps. Gorbachev's grandparents were victims and spent time in the Gulag labor camps. They were released in 1938 and returned home to tell stories of their suffering in the camps.

And as if the suffering under Stalin's ruthless regime was not enough, the Second World War broke out in 1939. Germany attacked the Soviet Union in 1941. During a short four and a half months in 1942, German troops occupied Privolnoe, where Gorbachev lived. At that time, Gorbachev's father, Sergey Andreyevich Gorbachev, was a soldier in the Soviet Red Army. At one point during the war, Sergey was declared dead, but he subsequently showed up.

One can only imagine the psychological impact that Stalin's terror and the World War had on Mikhail Gorbachev and millions of other children like him in the Soviet Union.

HISTORICAL SNAPSHOTS OF THE GREAT

Despite the disruption to his schooling caused by the war, Gorbachev achieved excellent academic performance. He was a voracious reader.

In 1946, while still in primary school, Mikhail Gorbachev joined a local youth political organization, Komsomol, and became the leader. He was even elected member of the district Komosol committee.

He subsequently joined high school in Molotovskeye. He was a very active member of the school. He was a member of the drama society and also led morning exercise classes.

Gorbachev helped his father on the farm during school holidays, sometimes working 20 hours a day harvesting grain.

In June 1950, at the age of 19, Mikhail Gorbachev joined Moscow State University (MSU) to study law. MSU was the most prestigious university in the Soviet Union at the time. Fellow students said that he worked extremely hard, sometimes studying into late hours of the night. He was outspoken in class and was also skillful in mediating disputes.

Mikhail Gorbachev was also active in politics while at law school. He held various leadership positions and became a full member of the Communist Party in 1952.

He met Raisa Titarenko, a philosophy student at MSU, and married her in September 1953.

Mikhail Gorbachev graduated from the university with a distinction in June 1955. He got a job at Stavropol. He continued studying via correspondence, obtaining a second degree in agricultural production from Stavropol Agricultural Institute in 1957.

He rose through the ranks in the local administration of Stavropol and gained credibility in the political establishment. He became extremely active in local Stavropol politics, rising in rank rapidly within Stavropol's political hierarchy. In 1968, he became the Second Secretary of the Stavropol Kraikom, the second most senior position in the Stavropol region. The following year he was elected deputy to the Supreme Soviet, the highest legislative body in the Soviet Union. In 1970, he was appointed to the highest political office in Stavropol, at a relatively young age of 39. This appointment meant that he would also become a member of the Central Committee of the Communist Party of the Soviet Union, which he joined in 1971, the "party elite." Gorbachev built close relationships with several influential figures within the political system in the Soviet Union.

In November 1978, he was appointed Secretary of the Central Committee. His stature within the party grew enormously. Over time, he gained access to leaders outside the country and built good relationships with them.

In March 1985, following the death of Chernenko, Mikhail Gorbachev, then 54, was unanimously elected by the Politburo to become the General Secretary of the Communist Party of the Soviet Union, the ruling party of the Soviet Union.

In 1985, after consolidating his power, Gorbachev started implementing a wide-ranging political and economic reform program, termed *perestroika*. The literal meaning of *perestroika* is restructuring. Key elements of *perestroika* were decentralization of economic planning, making state-owned businesses autonomous to operate as profit-making enterprises (although they were to remain state-owned), removing state price controls, and opening up the Soviet economy to foreign investment.

After introducing *perestroika,* Gorbachev ushered in *glasnost* in 1988, which means openness. Censorship of journalism was lifted. The policy also included reforms in the agricultural sector, ending the collectivization that had been in existence since the days of Joseph Stalin. In 1987, Gorbachev also introduced democracy, reducing the autocratic power of the Politburo.

Unfortunately, the results of *perestroika* and *glasnost* were mixed. There was an injection of capital from foreign investors, but the economy of the country tumbled. Government spending shot up, and inflation soared. Political opposition increased, destabilizing the country considerably. Many radicals emerged who were seeking more dramatic reforms. His political power started waning. Gorbachev eventually resigned after an unsuccessful *coup de etat* against him.

Although he presided over the collapse of the Soviet Union, Mikhail Gorbachev is regarded highly for the significant role he played in ending the Cold War, reducing civil rights abuse in the country, and helping remove Leninist/Marxist regimes in eastern Europe.

CHAPTER 11

Religion

*Science can purify religion from error and superstition.
Religion can purify science from idolatry and false
absolutes.*
—*Pope John Paul II*

RELIGIOUS FREEDOM HAD AN INTERESTING dimension at Naivasha Boarding School. Every student had the freedom to practice their faith. It just so happened that all students were Christians, albeit of different denominations.

On Sundays, students were allowed to go to their respective churches. For some students, the decision to go to a particular church was not a matter of faith. The decision was based on other factors such as access to shops where they could buy loaves of bread on the way back to school from the church. The distance of the church from the school was another important consideration. Generally, the further away from school, the more appealing it was because it meant more time for the student away from school. The aesthetic look of the church was another consideration. For example, the Anglican Church was a favorite of many students primarily because it was tucked away in a lovely leafy area of Naivasha. It was a delightful venue for worship.

Other considerations were the length of the church service (the shorter, the better) or the company that one would have on the way to and from the church. So, it was not surprising to find a student who was a Catholic on one Sunday and a follower of the Anglican Church the subsequent Sunday. It was all a matter of personal expediency.

One particular Sunday, my friend JK somehow discovered that he had relatives who lived very close to the Catholic Church. So, on that Sunday, both of us became Catholics so that we could visit the relatives after the church service. That would be a visit that would remain etched in my memory for many years.

We got to the house of JK's relative at around lunchtime. And near the main door to the house was a lady who was cooking pancakes in the open. The delicious aroma of the pancakes was overwhelming.

The relatives had not seen JK for many months, so we were welcomed into the house with immense joyousness. We only wished that the host would demonstrate his joy in an even more practical way by serving us with a few of the mouthwatering pancakes. However, this turned out to be a misplaced wish.

We waited, waited, and waited, but the pancakes never came.

Meanwhile, the host engaged JK on different topics ranging from the wellbeing of JK's siblings to the weather conditions in Nakuru the last time JK was at home in Nakuru.

After about an hour, it was time for the host to say goodbye to us. We went back to school, feeling ten times hungrier than if we had simply gone directly back to school immediately after the church service.

Later in life, after joining high school, I started gaining deep insights into religion. I remained a Christian, but this time I had an opportunity to interact with people from different religious backgrounds. I realized that although Christianity had the largest number of followers in the country, Islam and Hinduism had a significant presence in Nairobi and other large urban centers in Kenya.

During history lessons, I got a better understanding of the other religions and the key historical figures who were behind those religions.

It struck me that knowledge about other faiths was critical in ensuring peaceful co-existence amongst the people of this world. Also, if one was a true believer of their respective religion, then gaining some knowledge about other faiths would only strengthen their confidence in their religion.

As the Greek philosopher Epictetus (c. 55 – 135 AD) once said: "All religions must be tolerated… for every man must get to heaven in his own way." We will briefly explore the lives of the three people at the center of the three religions with the most substantial following in the world.

Jesus Christ

THE STORY OF JESUS CHRIST is fascinating and is at the core of the Christian faith. One of the fundamental beliefs of Christianity is that Jesus Christ was the Son of God.

According to the Old Testament of the *Bible*, the birth of Jesus Christ was foretold by Isaiah more than 700 years before the birth of Christ. Two verses in the book of Prophet Isaiah in the Old Testament contain this prophecy:

[14]Therefore the Lord himself shall give you a sign; Behold, a virgin shall conceive, and bear a son, and shall call his name, Immanuel.

– *Isaiah 7: 14*

[6]For unto us a child is born, unto us a son is given: and the government shall be upon his shoulder: and his name shall be called Wonderful, Counsellor, The mighty God, The everlasting Father, The Prince of Peace.

– *Isaiah 9: 6*

The books of Luke and Mathew in the New Testament of the Bible contain the story of the birth of Jesus Christ.

Jesus Christ was born in 4 AD in Bethlehem, Judea, a small rural town in the south of Jerusalem. The circumstances surrounding his birth were quite exceptional. His father, Joseph of Nazareth, had traveled to Bethlehem to participate in a census that was being conducted by the Roman government. However, due to overcrowding in Bethlehem at that time, Joseph could not find suitable accommodation. The only option available was an animal stable. He used the stable as a resting place for him and his family. The Bible says that his wife, the virgin Mary, gave birth to Jesus in the manger, surrounded by animals.

Word about the birth of Jesus Christ was spread around by herdsmen.

Several months after Jesus Christ was born, three wise men in Bethlehem learned about it. They followed the eastern star to trace the location of the birthplace of Jesus. They brought Joseph and Mary gifts of gold, frankincense, and myrrh.

King Herod of Judea, the Roman ruler at the time, heard of the birth of Jesus, who he was told would be the King of the Jews. Fearing the loss of power to the new-born Jewish King, King Herod ordered that all newly born Jewish boys in Bethlehem be killed.

The Bible says that Joseph learned about Herod's directive in a dream. After learning of the danger to Jesus, Joseph escaped to Egypt with his family.

While in Egypt, an angel of God appeared before Joseph and Mary. The angel told them that King Herod had died and that they should return to the Holy land. Joseph, Mary, and their child Jesus obeyed the orders. However, instead of going directly to Bethlehem, they went to Nazareth, in Galilee, to avoid the wrath of whoever was Herod's successor in Bethlehem.[39]

There is little literature that talks about the childhood of Jesus Christ. Theologians believe that he followed the footsteps of his father, Joseph, and became a carpenter.

Some scholars have speculated that Jesus Christ most probably underwent extensive tutelage from Jewish rabbis before bursting into the scene as a young adult. The scholars base this view on Jewish customs and traditions of the time, and the words in the book of Luke, Chapter 2 verse 22, which state that "Jesus grew in wisdom and stature, and in favor with God and men."

Other scholars suggest that Jesus Christ could have traveled extensively with his uncle Joseph of Arimathea, including travel to Glastonbury in Great Britain.

When Jesus was 30 years old, he was baptized in River Jordan by John the Baptist. After the baptism, Jesus went to the desert. He stayed there for several days. The Bible says that while he was in the desert, the devil tempted him several times, but he did not fall to the temptations.

After the 40 days in the desert, he returned to Bethlehem, where he started preaching the word of God.

In later years, Jesus went to Jerusalem. Large crowds met him shouting words of praise and referring to him as the King of Jews.

The Roman authorities heard about the arrival of Jesus Christ in Jerusalem. They were outraged and sent soldiers to search and apprehend and have him tried for blasphemy.

Meanwhile, Jesus Christ gathered his 13 disciples together. He told them that one of them would betray him to the Romans.

And indeed, as the Roman soldiers came searching for Jesus, Judas Iscariot, one of the disciples, kissed Jesus, making it obvious to the soldiers that he was kissing the Jesus that they were looking for. Judas was paid 30 coins of silver for this act of betrayal.

Jesus was then apprehended and handed over to the Jewish Elders, the Sanhedrin. The Sanhedrin sent Jesus to Pontius Pilate, governor of the Roman province of Judaea, for judgment. However, Pontius Pilate did not see any wrong-doing by Jesus Christ that warranted the death sentence. He ordered him flogged instead. However, the Sanhedrin was not happy with this punishment. Pilate acceded to their desires and ordered the crucifixion of Jesus Christ. Roman soldiers then escorted Jesus to Calvary, where he was hung on the cross until his death.

The Bible says that Jesus rose from the dead three days after his crucifixion and spoke to his followers. He asked them to pursue the virtues of love and forgiveness so that they could go to heaven upon leaving this earth.

The disciples of Jesus Christ continued to preach his message in Bethlehem and across many other lands.

There have been different interpretations of the Bible by various Christian denominations. Some ancient Jewish manuscripts (Dead Sea Scrolls) were discovered in 1947 in the Qumran Caves in the Judaean Desert near the Dead Sea. Experts are still deciphering the text in these scrolls. The scrolls that have been interpreted reveal a different image of Jesus from that presented in the Bible.

According to some scholars, weaving together the scrolls with other contextual historical information suggests that James, the uncle of Jesus, would have had better insights on the life of Jesus Christ than St. Paul, who wrote the book of

Luke, and the Apostle Mathew, who wrote the book of Mathew.

According to these scholars, the story of Jesus would have been as follows: (a) that Jesus was born naturally by Mary and not through a spiritual conception, (b) that Jesus was a charismatic preacher who also healed the sick, and, (c) that Jesus was a leader, who was recognized by Peter as the Jewish person who would bring liberation for the Jews from Roman domination. Further, (d) that Jesus was a leader who saw religion as intertwined with politics, and (e) that Jesus was a leader who rose from the dead to continue fighting for the liberation of the Jews.

However, there are questions around the veracity of the contents of the Dead Sea Scrolls. The critical point is that Paul's and Mathew's messages have withstood the test of time and made Christianity successful.

The core Christian beliefs are encapsulated in the Apostles' Creed used in liturgy by many Christian churches:

I believe in God,
the Father almighty,
Creator of heaven and earth,
and in Jesus Christ, his only Son, our Lord,
who was conceived by the Holy Spirit,
born of the Virgin Mary,
suffered under Pontius Pilate,
was crucified, died, and was buried;

he descended into hell;
on the third day he rose again from the dead;
he ascended into heaven,
and is seated at the right hand of God the Father almighty;
From there, he will come to judge the living and the dead.
I believe in the Holy Spirit,
the holy catholic Church,
the communion of saints,
the forgiveness of sins,
the resurrection of the body,
and life everlasting.
Amen.

The population of Christians in the world currently stands at approximately 2.1 billion. Nobody in the history of humanity has had such a substantial influence on people.

The Prophet Muhammad

IF WE WERE TO RANK the people who have had the most significant influence on human history, then Prophet Muhammad, peace be upon him, would rank amongst the ones at the very top of the list. He was born in Mecca and lived an ordinary life until age 40, when sudden changes in his life put into motion events that were to change history.

Muhammad was born in 570 AD in a poor family of the Quraysh tribe in Mecca. The name Muhammad means "Praiseworthy." His father, Abdullah, died before Muhammad was born.

When Muhammad was only a few months old, his mother, Aminah, handed him to a Bedouin wet nurse who stayed with him for four years in Arabia's deserts. This action was customary in the Qureshi tribe. The nurse returned Muhammad to his mother, Aminah, in 571 AD, but by that time, his mother was sickly. Aminah passed away after a short while. The responsibility for his upkeep was then transferred to his wealthy uncle, Abu Talib, when Muhammad was six years old.

Staying with his uncle allowed Muhammad to travel and interact with many people. At some point, he approached his uncle to allow him to marry one of his uncle's daughters. His uncle declined, citing Mohamed's lowly status as an orphan.

Subsequently, in a stroke of luck, Muhammad was sent on an errand by a wealthy widow, Khadija. He accomplished the errand successfully, making a good profit for Khadija. And in an unprecedented move, Khadija asked him to take her into marriage. Muhammad, although 16 years younger than her, accepted the offer. They stayed a happily married couple for the next 24 years when Khadija passed away after an illness.

At the age of 40, Muhammad started making regular visits to the hills around Mecca with his family. He would spend endless hours in the hills in meditation, sometimes days and nights. One night in the year 610, while sleeping in a cave in Mount Hira, a voice from the Angel Jibreel (Gabriel) asked Muhammad to read a written message. The voice asked him to read the message two times, but each time he responded that he could not read. The third time he was able to read.

Followers of Islam believe that the message that Muhammad read was directly from Allah. This message was the first of many subsequent divine revelations from Allah that were recorded in the Holy Qur'an by Muhammad's close acquaintances. [40] The literal translation of the *Qur'an* is "recitation."

The Qur'an has 144 chapters. Each chapter begins with the words *Bismillahir rahmanir Raheem* which translated means "In the name of Allah the most merciful and the most kind."

Muhammad spent the rest of his life conveying the messages in the Qur'an to people across Mecca and other distant places.

Initially, it was challenging for him to preach the Qur'an to the multiple tribes in Mecca, who believed in many different gods. People there did not entertain what Muhammad was teaching. The tribes feared that his teachings would affect commerce in Mecca, the place where various tribes came to worship their different gods.

The tribesmen of Mecca hatched a plot to assassinate Muhammad. But he escaped to Yathrib (present-day Medina) in the nick of time, from where he started spreading the Holy word of Allah through the Islam religion.

Followers of Islam refer to Muhammad's journey from Mecca to Yathrib as Hijrah. The Muslim calendar started from the date of this journey.

According to Islamic tradition, it is considered "*shirq*" (a corruption of Islam) to worship Muhammad. Islam requires all Muslims to worship Allah, the one and only true God (monotheism or "*tawhid*" in Arabic).

Depictions of Muhammad in any form whatsoever is prohibited. Unlike Christianity, where images depicting Jesus

Christ can be seen on display in churches, you can never find pictures or sculptures of Prophet Mohammed in any mosque. That is why Muslims across the world were outraged by the lampooning of the Prophet Muhammad in a French satirical weekly newspaper, *Charlie Hebdo*.

Two followers of the Muslim religion attacked the Paris offices of *Charlie Hebdo* offices on January 7, 2015, killing 12 people and injuring 11 others.

Apart from the *Qur'an*, Muslims use two other books, the *Hadith* and the *Sunnah*. The *Hadith* contains stories and sayings of Muhammad compiled after his death. The *Sunnah*, which means tradition, contains a biography (Sirah) of the Prophet Muhammad (or his way of life), which serves as a role model that Muslims should emulate.

Joining the Islamic faith is a free choice. One cannot join the religion through coercion.

Muslims believe that at one time, when Muhammad was asleep in the Kaaba in Mecca, he made a metaphysical journey to Jerusalem. Muslims refer to this journey as Muhammad's Night Journey. During the trip, Muhammad met and prayed with other previous prophets of God, going back to Abraham. While on the journey in Jerusalem, Muhammad climbed a ladder that took him through the seven heavens until he met Allah Himself. Allah gave him the single most important instruction, namely, that all followers of Islam must pray five times a day.

Muhammad's Night Journey marked the transition of Muhammad from a local Quraysh Muslim to a new phase of his life with a mission to spread the word of God to the whole of humanity.[41]

The final sermon at Mount Ararat captures the essence of the character of Prophet Muhammad. Below is an excerpt.[42]

> *All humanity is from Adam and Eve. An Arab has no superiority over a non-Arab, nor does a non-Arab have any superiority over an Arab; a white has no superiority over a black, nor does a black have any superiority over a white; [none have superiority over another] except by piety and good action.*
> *-Prophet Muhammad*

Muhammad died on June 8, 632 AD, while under the nursing care of Aisha, one of his wives.

Sri Krishna

HINDUISM IS THE THIRD-LARGEST religious denomination in the world, after Christianity and Islam. Hinduism has more than 1.2 billion followers, the majority of whom live in India. It is the oldest religious organization in recorded human history. The central figure in the Hindu religion is Sri Krishna.

Sri Krishna was born in 3228 BCE in a prison at Mathura, Uttar Pradesh, in the northern part of India. Uttar Pradesh is the most populous state in India today.

Sri Krishna was the eighth born in the family of Devaki and Vasudeva. At the time of his birth, Sri Krishna was under threat from Kamsa, the ruler of the Vrishni kingdom in which Mathura was located. Kamsa had been told that the eighth child of Devaki would kill him. So, he wanted to preempt this event by killing Sri Krishna.

Devaki and Vasudeva, realizing the immense imminent danger, smuggled their child, Sri Krishna, out of prison.

Sri Krishna was raised by foster parents, Nanda and Yasoda, in Gokula. He grew a healthy life in humble surroundings in a herding community. Indeed, he had his fair share of fun and mischief, just like any other child of his age at the time.

Many myths surround Krishna's life as a youngster. It is said that at one time, he lifted the Govardhana hill to protect the villagers. He is also said to have fought and slain the Trinavarta and Putana demons. Sri Krishna is also said to have played the flute to his devotees and taught them ways of self-realization.

Later in his life, Sri Krishna returned to Mathura, during which he killed Kamsa. The historical records describe various wars that occurred while Sri Krishna was in Mathura. During one of the wars, Sri Krishna issued the *Bhagavad Gita*, a 700-verse song, that became the scripture of the Hindu religion. *Bhagavad Gita* means the song of God.

The *Bhagavad Gita* is a profoundly philosophical text on the meaning of life. It contains practical advice on the actions that one should take to reach self-realization.[43]

The central messages of the Bhagavad Gita include selflessness and understanding the meaning of life to always strive towards positive action. Understanding the meaning of life requires understanding oneself from a spiritual and physical perspective. One also needs to understand the law of *karma,* which states that the results of one's actions will manifest themselves in the current or another life in the eternal cycle of life and death.

Understanding the meaning of life also requires one to understand the nature of God. The *Bhagavad Gita* describes God as the force behind all creation, in the eternal cycle of life that has no beginning or end. Understanding life also requires an appreciation of the illusion that clouds one's life perspectives and drives one to the trap of worldly desires that feed one's ego. Understanding the meaning of life also means appreciating one's higher purpose and having a union with God.

The *Bhagavad Gita* elucidates the four pathways of Yoga that lead to self-realization. Firstly, action through Karma Yoga, secondly, knowledge through Gyan Yoga, and thirdly, devotion through Bhakti Yoga. Finally, meditation through Raja Yoga.

The *Bhagavad Gita* also has many practical tips for leading a wholesome life, free of selfish desires, with the assurance of happiness and achievement of life's purpose.

Sri Krishna initially married eight wives with whom he bore many children. Later in his life, he took 16,100 women from the palace of Narakasura after killing Narakasura.

Sri Krishna retired in Dwarka, where he died in 1271 BCE after being shot in the ankle by a hunter who mistook him for a deer.

CHAPTER 12

Science and Technology

*Science and technology are a propellant for building a
thriving country, and the happiness of the people and
the future of the country hinge on their development.*

-Kim Jong-un

THE CHANGES OF PEOPLES' LIVES brought about by science and technology in recent years are phenomenal. It is hard to imagine that the television (TV), one of the most ubiquitous symbols of advancement brought about by science and technology, has been with us for just 95 years.

At Center, near Baharini, Nakuru, my childhood home, there was only one TV in the whole neighborhood. Mbote, who owned a bar just a few blocks from where we lived, was the owner of that TV.

Mbote had mounted his TV on a lockable shelf several feet above the floor behind the bar counter. The Voice of Kenya (VOK) was the sole TV station in the country.

Broadcasts by VOK started at 7:00 pm and ran for four hours. The final item on the TV was a ten-minute or so sermon and closing prayer by a Christian or Muslim religious leader.

Mbote would turn on the black-and-white TV at exactly 7:00 pm every day for the evening news. Many people flocked to the bar to buy drinks while enjoying the news broadcasts. However, the other people who could not afford the drinks just stood outside in a line watching the TV through the open door of the bar.

If a tall person happened to take a spot close to the door, then everyone else behind him was doomed – they just had to listen to the news without seeing the news broadcaster. In hindsight, this may not have been a significant disadvantage because most of the time, all that would appear on the screen was the person reading the news anyway, with minimal extra news footage.

On many occasions, Mbote would switch off the TV after the news broadcast, and the long line outside the bar would then disperse. The people outside would then head home in different directions discussing what they had just seen on TV.

After a few years, people started buying TVs for their homes and stopped relying on Mbote. The introduction of color television was a significant phenomenon. Only the relatively well-to-do families could afford such TVs. The color TV became a symbol of high social status.

Technology started entering our lives in multiple ways. Refrigerators, pressure cookers, and electric kettles started becoming common in homes. It would take several more years before such items could lose their perception as luxury goods for the elite and become common goods readily accessible by the general populace.

In 1968, when I moved to Naivasha Boarding School for my higher primary education, science and technology assumed a new dimension in my life. I found science lessons fascinating. However, there were times when, out of sheer mischief, some students went out of their way to beat technology. For example, some naughty students had discovered a foolproof way of avoiding homework and still have a watertight excuse to give to the teacher the following day.

All that the naughty students had to do was insert two metallic rods into the positive and negative outlets of one of the sockets in the classroom and then carefully place a third metallic rod on top of the two rods. Placing the third rod created a short-circuit and blew up the main fuse, creating total darkness in the whole school.

Nobody would know that the blackout was due to an act of mischief by some students. Prefects would ask students to go to the dormitory to sleep as there was no more light in the classrooms to facilitate studying.

When I joined high school in 1971, my interest in sciences grew even further as I gained exciting insights into how it all worked and the people behind it.

Some of the big names in science who continued to feed my imagination throughout my school years were the astronomers Leonardo da Vinci (1452 – 1519); Nicolaus Copernicus (1473 – 1543); Galileo Galilei (c. 1564 – 1642); Sir Isaac Newton, the mathematician and physicist (1642 – 1727); and the chemist Antoine Laurent Lavoisier (1743 – 1794). There were many others.

In later years, after leaving primary school, I came across other big names in science and technology whose ideas fascinated me immensely. Examples include Leonhard Euler (1707 – 1783) and Albert Einstein (1879-1955).

It would be interesting to explore the lives of some of these individuals who, along with others, had a significant influence on humanity during and even after their lives. We will look at Sir Isaac Newton, Leonhard Euler, and Albert Einstein.

Sir Isaac Newton

THE INFLUENCE OF SIR ISAAC NEWTON on humanity is almost impossible to describe. He walked onto the world stage and, through sheer intellect, made a massive impact on human affairs. I would argue that virtually every high school graduate across the entire globe must have encountered Isaac Newton in their studies at one time or another. What is even more phenomenal is the wide-ranging spheres of his influence in science and technology. It is truly amazing.

Sir Isaac Newton was born at Woolsthorpe village, Lincolnshire, England, on Christmas day in 1642. He was born in a family of modest means. He was born prematurely as a tiny baby. He was weak and not expected to survive.[44]

His father, also named Isaac Newton Snr, died three months before Isaac Newton was born.

When Newton was three years old, his mother, Hannah Ayscough, married another man, the Reverend Barnabus Smith. She left Isaac Newton under the care of his maternal grandmother, Margery Ayscough.

Isaac Newton attended local schools in Lincolnshire until the age of 12, when he joined King's School in Grantham, England, where he studied Latin, Greek, and Mathematics.

During his time at King's School, Isaac Newton lived with a pharmacist called Clark. He used Clark's chemical library and laboratory, at times building small mechanical contraptions for Clark's daughter. It would appear that it was in that environment that Isaac Newton developed his interest in the physical sciences.

When Reverend Barnabus Smith, Newton's stepfather, died in October 1659, Newton's mother removed Newton from school. He was 12 years old at that time. She asked Newton to work on the family farm at Woolsthorpe. However, Isaac Newton was not interested in farming. Fortunately, following the intervention of his school headmaster, Henry Stokes, Newton was able to return to Grantham in 1660 to continue with his schooling.

Isaac Newton completed high school with excellent grades. He was admitted to Trinity College, Cambridge in England to study law. His life challenges followed him at Cambridge. He worked there as a waiter and house cleaner as he pursued his degree. When he was in his third year at university, his interest shifted to mathematics and natural philosophy (physics). He was not an exceptional student. His grades were just average. After three years, he earned a four-year scholarship, which enabled him to focus on his studies full-time.

In 1665, when Isaac Newton was only 22 years old, he made his first significant mathematical discovery in mathematics, the generalized binomial theorem. He graduated with a BA in Natural Philosophy in the same year.

An outbreak of the bubonic plague in 1665 forced the university to close down and disrupted Newton's studies. The closure of the university was a blessing in disguise because it allowed Newton to spend time at home pondering some ground-breaking ideas in mathematics, physics, optics, and astronomy.

By 1666, Isaac Newton came up with novel ideas regarding motion, namely, the three laws of motion:

1. *An object will not change its motion unless a force acts on it.*
2. *The force on an object is equal to its mass times its acceleration.*
3. *When two objects interact, they apply forces to each other of equal magnitude and opposite direction.*[45]

In 1667, Newton returned to Cambridge after a two-year hiatus. He continued with his post-graduate studies and graduated with a Master of Arts degree in 1669.

In subsequent years, Newton made other breakthroughs in Mathematics and Physics. Some of his discoveries included the first reflecting telescope, calculus, and the laws of gravity.

His book, the *Principia*, first published in 1687, would remain a masterpiece in mathematics and scientific circles for many years. It was a complex book that many scientists did not fully understand when it was first published.

Isaac Newton was a secretive, profoundly introverted, and private person. He also displayed traits of being a little insecure and sometimes burst into a temper of fury. There is a time in

1693 when he spent five days without sleeping and almost got a nervous breakdown.

An anecdotal insight into the softer side of Isaac Newton's character can be discerned from a note that he wrote in 1662 (Fitzwilliam Notebook) addressed directly to God in which he listed all the sins that he had committed.[46] Some of the sins listed in the notebook included:

> *Eating an apple at Thy house*
> *Making a mousetrap on Thy day*
> *Making pies on Sunday night*
> *Robbing my mothers box of plums and sugar*
> *Caring for worldly things more than God."*

Newton died in his sleep in London on March 20, 1727.

Leonhard Euler

I BELIEVE THAT LEONHARD EULER has never received the recognition that he deserves. He is the one who came up with the Euler identity, a mathematical equation that has never ceased to fascinate me.

He was a prolific writer, contributing approximately 30% of all works in mathematics published in the 18th Century. Some of his works were being published long after his death. He was a man of extraordinary intellect. He is No.1 in my subjective list of geniuses.

◆◆◆

Leonhard Euler was born in Switzerland, in the town of Basel on April 15, 1707. He was born into a deeply religious family. His father, Paul III Euler, was a pastor of the Reformed Church, while his mother, Marguerite née Brucker, was the daughter of a pastor. Leonhard Euler himself led a long-standing Christian life.

The Euler family moved to a town called Riehen, in the canton of Basel-Stadt, when Euler was one year old. He spent most of his childhood there.

Later on, Euler went to a school in Basel, where he lived with his maternal grandmother. He joined the University of Basel in 1720 when he was 13 years old. Three years later, he graduated with a Master of Philosophy degree. The focus of his study was the philosophy of Rene Descartes and Isaac Newton, both of whom were renowned scholars in mathematics and science.

While studying for his Philosophy degree, Leonhard Euler pursued private studies in Mathematics over the week-ends, under the guidance of the great mathematician John Bernoulli, a great friend of his father. In his autobiography, Euler stated that Bernoulli was usually very busy. Still, he encouraged Euler to read challenging books in mathematics independently and reach out to him if he encountered any difficulties. Further, that Bernoulli allowed Euler to visit him every Sunday afternoon for an explanation of any difficult concepts that Euler may have encountered[47].

The next phase of Leonard Euler's education was theology to become a pastor. However, John Bernoulli had noticed his talent in mathematics. He convinced Euler's father that the young Euler should pursue a different course rather than pursuing studies to become a clergyman.

Leonhard Euler finished his studies at the University of Basel in 1726. He traveled to St. Petersburg in Russia the following year to take up a post at St. Petersburg Academy of Sciences.

At the St Petersburg Academy, Euler was surrounded by eminent scientists, including Jakob Hermann (a Swiss mathematician who made significant contributions in dynamics); Christian Goldbach (a guru in number theory); Maier (a specialist in trigonometry); and J-N Delisle (a geographer and an astronomer).

Between 1727 and 1730, Leonhard Euler worked as a medical lieutenant in the Russian navy.

In 1730, he became a full-time professor of physics at the St Petersburg Academy of Sciences. He married Katharina

Gsell in January 1734, with whom he got 13 children. Only five of them survived through infancy.

While holding his position at the Academy, he did extensive research in different areas of mathematics, notably number theory, infinitary analysis, differential equations and the calculus of variations, and rational mechanics. He published numerous articles. He also won different prestigious prizes in mathematics.

In June 1741, Leonhard Euler left the St Petersburg Academy of Sciences and traveled to Berlin at the invitation of Frederick the Great. He joined the Academy of Science in Berlin. He also carried out a wide range of duties for the king, ranging from supervising botanical gardens to managing work on pumps and pipes of the hydraulic system at Sans Souci, the summer residence of the royal family.

Despite the multiple duties in Berlin, Euler continued his academic work. During the 25 years that he stayed in Berlin, he wrote about 380 articles. He also wrote books on diverse subjects, including calculus of variations, calculation of planetary orbits; artillery and ballistics; analysis; shipbuilding and navigation; the motion of the moon; and lectures on differential calculus.

Euler returned to St. Petersburg in 1766. By that time, he had already started developing blindness. He became totally blind in 1771. The remarkable thing is that despite his blindness, he continued to be productive, with the assistance of his two sons and other scientists.

It is incredible that after his death in 1783, the "St Petersburg Academy continued to publish Euler's unpublished work for nearly 50 more years."[48]

The enormity of Euler's contributions to mathematics is legendary. He brought us the notations f(x) for a function, e for the base of natural logarithms, i for the square root of -1, π for pi, $\sum$ for summation, the notation for finite differences Δy and $\Delta 2y$, and many others. The sheer volume of his contributions is mind-boggling.

It would be remiss of me to conclude Euler's story without presenting one of the most beautiful and fascinating mathematical equations that I have ever come across. The Euler identity, which Leonhard Euler developed in 1748, is an equation that links five fundamental mathematical constants:

$$e^{i\pi} + 1 = 0$$

e – the number that underlies exponential growth

i – the "imaginary" square root of -1

$$\sqrt{4} = 2$$
$$\sqrt{-1} = i$$

π or pi – the ratio of the circumference of a circle to its diameter

1 – the basis of all other numbers

0 – the concept of nothingness

In a poll of readers conducted by The Mathematical Intelligencer in 1990, readers said that Euler's identity was the most beautiful mathematical equation ever.[49]

What a genius?

Albert Einstein

I WOULD LIKE TO MAKE some claims that cannot be empirically proven, but which many readers will probably agree with. Firstly, I believe that almost everyone who has graduated from high school has heard of Albert Einstein. Secondly, I believe that most of these people have heard of Albert Einstein referred to as a genius in science.

Indeed, the bearded image of Albert Einstein has almost become a universal symbol of genius. And that symbolism is something that I believe is well-deserved by the man.

Albert Einstein published more than 450 papers, 300 of which were scientific, and the other 150 non-scientific. He was awarded a Nobel Prize in Physics in 1921. But who was this man, and how did he accomplish such a fantastic feat in human history?

Albert Einstein was born on March 14, 1879, to working-class Jewish parents, in Ulm, Germany. His father, Hermann

Einstein, was a salesman and engineer, while his mother, Pauline Koch, took care of the household. Hermann moved the family to Munich in 1880.

When Einstein reached age five, he joined a Catholic elementary school in Munich. He stayed there for three years, then transferred to Luitpold Gymnasium, where he continued with his primary and secondary school education.

Einstein never enjoyed his schooling at the Gymnasium, which he felt stifled creativity and originality. One of the teachers there even told him that he would become a failure in life. Einstein once wrote that:

School failed me, and I failed the school. It bored me. The teachers behaved like sergeants. I wanted to learn what I wanted to know, but they wanted me to learn for the exam. What I hated most was the competitive system there, and especially sports. Because of this, I wasn't worth anything, and several times they suggested I leave.[50]

There were two significant influences in Einstein's early life. The first one was the discovery of a compass, which fascinated him because of the way it worked using invisible forces. The second one was discovering a book on geometry, which he read from cover to cover. The book opened up his mind to the fascinating world of mathematics.

Max Talmud, a young medical student who used to visit the Einsteins for dinner, introduced Einstein to higher mathematics and philosophy. Talmud also introduced Einstein to a children's science book series by Aaron Bernstein. Einstein later said that these books shaped his thinking on light.[51]

When Einstein was 16, his parents moved to Milan, Italy, to look for better pastures as the business in Munich had floundered. Einstein was left in Berlin to finish his secondary school education. However, six months later, he left school and followed his parents in Italy. Einstein's arrival in Milan posed a big challenge for his parents because he did not have a high school diploma.

Fortunately, it turned out that Einstein could apply to join the Swiss Federal Institute of Technology without a high school diploma, on condition that he passed the entrance examinations. He sat the exams and obtained exceptionally high scores in mathematics and physics. His French, chemistry, and biology scores were poor, but he was accepted because of his high scores in maths and physics. Still, his entry into the university was conditional upon first finishing secondary school.

Einstein joined an Argovian cantonal school (Gymnasium) in Aarau, Switzerland, and graduated in 1896. He also renounced his German citizenship in the same year to avoid military service. He became a Swiss citizen in 1901.

Einstein passed his final secondary school examinations with excellent grades in maths and physics; and reasonable grades in the other subjects. He then joined Zürich Polytechnic to study for a four-year diploma in teaching, specializing in mathematics and physics. He met his future Serbian wife Mileva Marić there, a fellow student at the university. Einstein graduated with a teaching diploma in 1900.

After graduation, Einstein experienced a hard time finding a teaching job, primarily because of a poor relationship with his professors. He had skipped many classroom lessons, preferring to pursue his studies independently.

After two years of joblessness, he found a job in the Swiss patent office. He continued studying while working at the patent office. He wrote several ground-breaking academic papers that bolstered his reputation in academic circles.

He completed his Ph.D. in 1905. The title of his thesis was "A New Determination of Molecular Dimensions."

Einstein wrote four academic articles that put his career on a new trajectory. The articles were published in the prestigious peer-reviewed scientific journal *Annalen der Physik*. Two of the articles were on Brownian motion and the photoelectric effect. The other two were on special relativity and introduced the famous concept $e = mc^2$.

Einstein's subsequent work propelled him to new heights in academic circles. His career blossomed exponentially. He gained worldwide fame for his genius. He also traveled widely.

In 1933, Einstein joined the Institute for Advanced Study at Princeton, New Jersey, in the USA. He became a USA citizen in 1940.

Although not directly involved, Einstein was instrumental in the development of the atomic bomb at the Manhattan Project. He later expressed regret at having been involved with the development of the weapon.

Einstein died on April 18, 1955, at age 76 at the University Medical Center at Princeton, after an illustrious career as a scientist of unparalleled genius.

CHAPTER 13

Sports

Float like a butterfly, sting like a bee. His hands can't hit what his eyes can't see. Now you see me, now you don't. George thinks he will, but I know he won't.
—Mohammed Ali

I AM CONVINCED THAT THERE are many world-class athletes that I met in primary school and in high school who just disappeared unnoticed, simply because they were not fortunate enough to find a suitable platform to demonstrate their skills for the world to see. For example, there was Amos Kinuthia, who was two years ahead of me at Naivasha Boarding School. He was of medium height with a broad chest that was probably a secret chamber for a human engine more efficient than that of a modern-day sports car. I can bet that if he had been given the opportunity, he would have been in the league of the likes of Usain Bolt. He was always competing for the school in the district and provincial events, and he won most of the time.

There was Josphat too. He was a boy from the highlands of Central Kenya. He had hands that moved faster than the needles of an automatic sewing machine. He was an extraordinary boxer who sometimes took on boys almost twice his size and felled them comfortably on the ring.

At the beginning of the first boxing round, Josphat would spring on his thin legs for a few minutes, ducking from time to time as his opponent tried to punch him. However, at a strategic moment, the young Josphat would unleash a set of blows in quick succession that would disorient his opponent. If the opponent was a much bigger boy, then the pain of the blows would be exacerbated by the sense of imminent defeat, compounded ten-fold by the screams and laughter of the audience.

Typically, the boxing matches would be one of the after-supper activities on Saturday nights. And Josphat almost always gave a performance that would engage students for another few days depending upon the size of the opponent whom he had humiliated.

I never got to know where Josphat went after primary school. Still, the chances are that he just became an ordinary high school student somewhere in Kenya, where his talent as a boxer was probably never recognized.

I believe that Josphat had what it took to become a great boxing athlete. A great athlete like Muhammad Ali, one of the most charismatic and successful boxers in recent years.

Muhammad Ali

MUHAMMAD ALI MUST COUNT AS one of the greatest athletes who ever lived. His charisma invoked tremendous appeal among people of all age groups, irrespective of their socio-economic status.

Muhammad Ali lifted the game of boxing to levels that had not been seen before. I would argue that there is no other boxer who has had such a significant influence on people's imagination as he did. He was truly inspirational.

It would be interesting to examine the early life of Muhammad Ali to understand how he became the "greatest." As he used to say, "I am the greatest; I said that even before I knew I was."

Muhammad Ali was born Cassius Marcellus Clay on January 17, 1942, in Louisville, Kentucky. He renounced his name Cassius Clay on June 30, 1967.

Muhammad Ali was born in a family of modest means. He was born when there was deep racial segregation in America, something that must have shaped his character in later life.

His father, Cassius Marcellus Clay Sr., was a sign and billboard painter and musician. In 1971, a New York Times reporter described Cassius Marcellus Clay as "a handsome, mercurial, noisy, combative failed dreamer."[52]

Muhammad Ali's mother, Odessa O'Grady Clay, worked as a domestic servant.

Muhammad Ali went to Virginia Avenue Elementary School and subsequently to Louisville Central High School in Louisville, Kentucky. His performance was nothing to write home about, except for art and gym.[53]

His entry into the boxing world was interesting. When he was 12 years old, somebody stole his $60 bicycle. In a fit of rage, Ali went looking for a police officer to help catch the thief. He met a policeman who was teaching boxing to some boys from the neighborhood. Ali asked the police officer to help Ali find the thief so that he could "whup" the thief. The police officer, Joe E. Martin, asked Ali first to join the boxing class. Ali joined the boxing class.[54]

Muhammad Ali enjoyed boxing as it provided him with an avenue to expend his enormous youthful energy and gain the constant recognition he craved. He worked hard at it. He used unconventional techniques, but his coach did not try to change him. His incredible speed offset the shortcomings in technique.

Muhammad Ali fought many amateur bouts successfully. He won a gold medal in the light heavyweight division at the 1960 Summer Olympics. He turned into a professional boxer later that year.

In 1961, Muhammad Ali joined the Muslim religion and changed his name from Cassius Clay to Muhammad Ali.

A significant turning point in his professional boxing career occurred in 1964, at age 22, when he defeated a ferocious opponent Sonny Liston, to become the world's heavyweight boxing champion.

Liston had a criminal record and connections with the mob. Most people expected Ali to lose to Liston. However, Muhammad Ali was unfazed. In his characteristic fashion, he taunted Sonny Liston at the weigh-in before the fight. The words that Muhammad Ali used are quite telling. He called Liston "the big ugly bear." He said that "Liston even smells like a bear." He added: "After I beat him, I'm going to donate him to the zoo." He shouted at Liston, "someone is going to die at ringside tonight." Muhammad Ali won the fight despite being the underdog going into the ring.

Muhammad Ali's career grew phenomenally after that fight.

Later in his life, he became a controversial figure due to his involvement with Malcolm X and the Nation of Islam, as well as his refusal to join the army to go to Vietnam. These events would have a significant toll on his career as a boxer. Eventually, he made it through and managed to leave a unique legacy as one of the world's greatest fighters before his death in Scottsdale, Arizona, on June 2, 2016, at the ripe age of 74 years.

Many people retain fond memories of Ali's trademark taunts before boxing bouts. For example, in 1974, in an interview with the press before a major highly publicized fight with George Foreman in Zaire (Ramble in the Jungle as the fight was dubbed), Muhammad Ali told David Frost:

> *If you think the world was surprised when Nixon resigned, wait 'til I whup Foreman's behind! I've done something new for this fight. I done wrestled with an alligator, I done tussled with a whale; handcuffed lightning, thrown thunder in jail; only last week, I murdered a rock, injured a stone, hospitalized a brick; I'm so mean I make medicine sick.*

May Muhammad Ali's soul rest in peace.

CHAPTER 14

Writing

*Everyone thinks of changing the world, but no one
thinks of changing himself.*
— Leo Tolstoy

I F THERE IS SOMETHING THAT I enjoyed about my
life at Naivasha Boarding School, it was the opportunity
that I got to read novels. And not all types of novels, but
novels by James Hadley Chase.

James Hadley Chase novels were so thrilling that I could
hardly put one down after I had started reading it. I must have
read more than 30 of his novels, some within less than a week
- in between classes, after classes, and during weekends. Many
other students shared my passion for James Hadley Chase
novels.

Teachers discouraged us from reading James Hardley
Chase's novels. Nobody ever explained to me the underlying

reason for this discouragement. I assumed it was to do with the language that James Hadley Chase used in his novels, a language that was miles apart from the language used in the set books that we used in English language classes. But if a language is intended to communicate, then surely, James Hadley Chase knew how to communicate and catch one's attention.

Perhaps the teachers discouraged us from reading James Hadley Chase novels because of the nature of the books' contents. The stories were pure thrillers and encompassed blackmail, murder, love, jealousy, double-crossing, and greed. There was also a sprinkling of sex in some novels, presented in a civilized manner.

Perhaps teachers did not want us to indulge in the novels lest James Hadley Chase influenced us to act out some of the unpleasant things that he described in the books. But if that were the reason, then I would argue that it was a misplaced fear. There is hardly a book that I can think of that is highly regarded that does not contain one of these things. I would argue that it is the writers who narrate events around these topics effectively that end up becoming highly regarded in society.

It is difficult to determine the writers who have had the most significant influence on society in general, partly because writing cuts across many disciplines. A writer of memoirs may be classified as a good philosopher. An excellent writer of fictional books may be classified as a good writer of English literature.

For purposes of this book, we will examine two writers listed in Biography Online as among the top 100 people who have had the most significant influence on society. These are the Russian writer Leo Tolstoy and the American writer Earnest Hemingway.

Leo Tolstoy

LEO TOLSTOY BECAME FAMOUS FOR writing two epic novels, War & Peace and Anna Karenina. These are novels written about human experiences in an extremely absorbing fashion. Stories that conjure up different emotions in the reader to the extent that at the end of the story, the reader wishes that the novel would just continue without an ending.

Leo Tolstoy received nominations for the Nobel Prize in Literature several times. But who was he?

Leo Tolstoy was born on September 9, 1828, in Yasnaya Polyana, Tula Province, Russia. He was born into a powerful family of Russian aristocrats. He was the fourth child of

Count Nikolai Ilyich Tolstoy and Countess Mariya Tolstaya. His mother passed away when he was two years old. His father died seven years later. Tolstoy then grew up under the care of his aunts.

Tolstoy's early education was exceptional. He was tutored at home by French and German teachers until he was ready to go to university. He joined the University of Kazan, Russia, in 1843, at the age of 15 to study Oriental languages, which would have suited him well in his ambition to pursue a career in diplomacy. However, his performance in languages was weak, forcing him to switch to law, which was more manageable.

While at university, Tolstoy was a party animal. He left the University of Kazan after four years without graduating. He returned to his parents' farm to try farming. Farming did not work well for him, either. He spent most of his time in the city socializing with people. When he went back home, he started keeping a journal, which would mark the starting point of his lifelong vocation as a writer.

In November 1854, Tolstoy joined the army. He continued writing when he was in the military. He started by writing a story about his childhood. The title of that work was *Childhood*. He wrote several other works in quick succession, including *Boyhood, Sevastopol Tales, a three-part series*. He also wrote about his life in the army, which he completed in 1862 after leaving the military. The title of this book was *The Cossacks*.

By the time Tolstoy left the army, he had already gained recognition in literary circles in Russia. However, he was a law unto himself, refusing to align himself with the status quo in literature.

In 1857 he left for Paris, where he spent time enjoying himself. He also got involved in gambling, during which he lost a lot of money. After becoming broke, he returned to Russia, where he started publishing for the journal *Yasnaya Polyana*. Later that year, he married Sophia Andreevna Behrs, who was 16 years younger than him. Sofya was to become an essential partner in his writing career, working effectively as his secretary, editor, and financial manager.

When he was in *Yasnaya Polyana*, he started writing the novel *War and Peace*. Some chapters of the novel were published in 1865. A few more chapters were published in 1868. He completed the book in 1869. The book was fictional but was rich with the history of Russia during the war years. The novel was a great success.

Tolstoy followed *War and Peace* with *Anna Karenina*, a compelling fictional romance novel that was also published in parts between 1873 to 1877. The new book was also successful and earned Tolstoy a lot of money.

Tolstoy underwent a personal spiritual crisis, which sometimes caused a clash between him and the church and his wife. This turmoil continued throughout old age.

He continued writing and producing, including another successful work of fiction, *The Death of Ivan Ilyich*, in 1886. He wrote extensively during the 1880s, and in later years, earning the admiration of such great figures as Mahatma Gandhi and Martin Luther King, Jnr.

The two trips that he made out of Russia had a significant influence on Tolstoy's world and shaped his writing career. The first visit was in 1857, when he traveled to France and witnessed first-hand the brutality that was being meted out by the French government to its citizens. Tolstoy vowed never to work for the government in his life. The second trip was to Europe in 1860/61, during which he met Victor Hugo, the author of *Les Miserables*, and Pierre-Joseph Proudhon, an influential anarchist who was living in exile in Belgium.

Tolstoy died on November 20, 1910, at 82 years, at a railroad station in Astapovo, while on a pilgrimage that proved too strenuous for his health.

Ernest Hemingway

ERNEST HEMINGWAY IS ONE OF the most celebrated American writers. He had a unique writing style that endeared him to many readers across the world. He was the author of several best-selling novels, including *For Whom the Bell Tolls*, *The Old Man and the Sea*, and *The Sun Also Rises*.

Hemingway wrote numerous other books. He was awarded the Pulitzer Prize in Literature in 1953. And in 1954, he won the Nobel Prize in Literature

Ernest Hemingway was born on July 21, 1899, in Oak Pak, Illinois, near Chicago. He was the second-born among six children of well-educated parents, Clarence Edmonds Hemingway, a physician, and Grace Hall Hemingway, an opera singer, music teacher, and painter. His father was a perfectionist.

Ernest Hemingway was born with a slight speech defect and a problem with eyesight, which affected his writing career.

When he was a young boy, Ernest Hemingway used to join his parents on weekend trips to the countryside in the northern woods of Michigan, where the family would do fishing, hunting, camping, vegetable gardening, and other adventurous things. During Earnest Hemingway's third and fourth birthdays, the gift from his father was an all-day trip to Lake Michigan for fishing. And on his 12th birthday, the gift from his grandfather was a single-barrel 20-gauge gun.[55]

Earnest Hemingway attended Oak Park and River Forest High School from 1913 to 1917. He was keen on sports and participated in boxing, track and field, water polo, and football. He performed exceptionally well in English classes.

He was also active in writing when in High school. He wrote for the school's newspaper, *The Trapeze*, and also published articles for the literary magazine *The Tabula*.

Ernest Hemingway's mother, a deeply religious woman, was keen on instilling Christian values on her son, but her efforts had the opposite effect.

Ernest Hemingway did not go to college after finishing high school. He had no interest in higher education. His father found him an opening at the *Kansas City Star* as a reporter. It was there where he was taught how to write in short sentences, avoiding clichés and unnecessary adjectives in his stories. Six months after joining the *Kansas City Star,* Ernest Hemingway left for New York to join the army. He was keen on participating in the war.

After recruitment by the army, Ernest Hemingway traveled to the theatre of the war in Europe, starting with Italy, where he witnessed the war in action first-hand. He received wounds on his leg and kneecap, forcing him to return to the USA. Some writers have indicated that the near-death experience at the war front in the border of Italy and Austria was the primary driver of Ernest Hemingway's writing in subsequent years.

After the war, Ernest Hemingway lived a colorful life full of ups and downs in different parts of the world. An amusing anecdote is of a time when after returning to Europe, Hemingway was asked by the *Toronto Star* to cover the

Lausanne Peace Conference. While in Lausanne, he asked his wife Hadley to join him. She carried all his book manuscripts in her luggage, including the carbon copies. Unfortunately, the case in which she had packed these documents was stolen at Lyon train station, a monumental loss for Hemingway. But this loss did not discourage him. He sustained his writing career, which continued to blossom, reaching a peak in 1953 and 1954 when he earned the Pulitzer Prize in Literature and the Nobel Prize in Literature, respectively. These were accomplishments that most writers could only dream of.

Ernest Hemingway married and divorced several times. He was afflicted with high blood pressure and continuous depression in the twilight years of his life. Deteriorating health resulted in his extended confinement in hospital at the Mayo Clinic in Rochester, Minnesota. He died on July 2, 1961, after shooting himself. America and the world lost one of the best literary brains ever.

PART TWO

How did they do it?

CHAPTER 15

Bringing it all Together

Believe in yourself. You are braver than you think,
more talented than you know, and capable of more
than you imagine.
— Roy T. Bennet

I T IS REASONABLE TO PROCEED from the premise
that there is no one size fits all in terms of the attributes
that make a person great. Firstly, there are significant
differences in the dynamics that drive success in the various
life domains. For example, becoming a hero in the military
depends on totally different factors from becoming a hero in
art. Secondly, historical contexts may be different too. For
example, if you were born in the 21st Century and possessed
the "red hot genes" of an explorer, you are unlikely to discover
new continents irrespective of your courage. However, you
could gain enormous fame, even greater than that of
Christopher Columbus, by exploring outer space. Thirdly,
there are social and cultural differences to consider. For

example, if one were born somewhere deep in the Congo forest where schooling is probably non-existent, then chances of discovering differential calculus as Issac Newton did would be very slim. However, there would be opportunities for gaining fame in the far reaches of the Congo forest by discovering a medicinal plant that could cure malaria. All these different factors make it difficult to draw general conclusions about the drivers of greatness.

On the other hand, the analytical challenges described above are also an opportunity because, if one can apply some rigor and find common attributes of those who rose to greatness, they would have discovered a real gem. A gem that could assist humanity in nurturing the young upcoming generation into individuals who can propel the world into greater heights of prosperity. Not only that. It would provide a blueprint for everyone who wishes to excel in their particular vocation. The quest to discover such a gem is the spirit in which we will discuss the underlying personal attributes that contributed to the greatness of the individuals presented in this book.

CHAPTER 16

A Matter of Luck

*I think we consider too much the good luck of the early
bird and not enough the bad luck of the early worm.*
— *Franklin D. Roosevelt*

S OME PEOPLE ARE JUST BORN lucky. When I
think about luck, it reminds me of a former schoolmate
called Caleb. Nature had conspired to make Caleb one
of the most fortunate boys at Naivasha Boarding School.

I joined Naivasha Boarding School in 1968, four years after
Kenya gained independence. The mood in the country at that
time was upbeat. Politics was in the air, everywhere, even in a
school of young boys such as Naivasha Boarding School.
During civics lessons at the school, we learned in detail how
the Kenya government was structured. We were even required
to memorize the names of members of the cabinet and their
assistants; and similar mundane information. There was a
deliberate attempt to instill patriotism in all students.

At that time, people who held senior government positions were greatly respected. The respect extended to members of their families too. It was something akin to the respect accorded to members of the monarchy in some countries. Students respected any student who had a connection with a senior government official. One such student was Caleb, whose father was a member of the Presidential Escort.

At the time, the President of Kenya, President Jomo Kenyatta, spent a lot of his time at the State House in Nakuru. He traveled quite frequently between the capital city Nairobi and Nakuru town. He went mainly by road and therefore had to pass by Naivasha many times (Naivasha is about halfway between Nairobi and Nakuru).

It was customary that when the President passed through Naivasha, all schools in Naivasha town would be shut down so that students could go to town to welcome him.

Students would stand on the side of the road for several hours, waiting for the President to arrive. Several teams of traditional dancers would provide entertainment, which created a certain vibrancy in the atmosphere and added color to the occasion.

The eventual arrival of the President was a major spectacle. Firstly, six or so powerful motorcycles would drive into the town at high speed, signaling that the President was just a few minutes behind. About five black limousines carrying members of the President's security personnel would then emerge shortly after that.

The limousines had big red number plates written "Presidential Escort." Mean-looking security personnel adorned in black suits would then alight from the limousines and start running in-front slowly and along the sides of the limousines, making sure that the road was clear and there were no security threats. Some of the security personnel would mingle with people waiting on the side of the road.

The President's black stretch limousine sandwiched between other black limousines would then appear. The President's limousine would have two beautiful flags at the front, the Kenyan flag on the front left-hand side, and the President's flag on the right-hand side.

The sight of President Jomo Kenyatta sitting majestically in the limousine filled one with tremendous awe.

The President would then alight from his limousine at a strategic point after entering the main Naivasha town center. Local senior government officials and other senior members of the ruling party would be on standby to greet him as he alighted from the vehicle. He would then walk for several meters in the company of the officials, waving his trademark flywhisk, as hundreds of people on the side of the road shouted in jubilation. Traditional dancers would dance vigorously to impress the President. Occasionally, he would stop briefly to appreciate the dancers.

After walking for about 100 meters, the President would then get into his limousine, open the sunroof, and then give a brief address to the people gathered around. After the short speech, the President would issue his rallying call: "Harambee," and people would respond: "Hooo." He would make the call three times, and then shut the sunroof of his vehicle, then continue on his journey to Nakuru, sandwiched between his impressive motorcade of presidential escorts, security personnel, the presidential press unit, and other government officials.

The convoy would move at high speed, a phenomenon that would be the subject of animated discussion by students as they headed back to school.

The brief visit by the president was always an impressive show that students never wanted to miss.

Amidst all the hullaballoo, as people were shouting and waving for the President, Caleb would find his way through the crowd and the security men to reach his father in one of the presidential escort limousines. After a brief chat, his father would always give Caleb a small amount of money.

Caleb would buy sweets and snacks on the way back to school, which he would share with friends. He was a lucky student indeed. Many students envied him.

And just because other students had seen Caleb speaking to his father next to the impressive-looking limousine, Caleb acquired a certain aura of importance. He received special attention and favors from prefects and teachers. He was lucky to be the son of a member of the Presidential Escort.

When we look at the stories of some of the most influential figures in world history narrated in this book, we also see several instances of individuals who were just born lucky. One could attribute their greatness partly due to the sheer circumstances of their birth or other external factors that worked in their favor, and in some instances, circumstances that worked horribly against them. We can cite a few examples to illustrate this point.

If you take a person like Malcolm X, he was unlucky to be born black at a time when the white race hated black people. He found himself in circumstances that transformed him into a criminal, leading to his incarceration.

But Malcolm X was lucky too because when he landed in jail, he found himself surrounded by books, books that he read voraciously. It is evident from his autobiography that the books opened up his mind, leading to his second transformation into a great political activist.

Another example is Michelangelo. If Bertoldo di Giovani had not spotted him when he was an art apprentice in Florence, then the world would probably never have known of Michelangelo's talent in sculpturing and painting. Even Henry Ford was lucky to get people who were willing to give him financial backing to set up the Ford Motor Company in 1903. He would probably have ended up living an ordinary life in Detroit if he did not receive that financial support. And the cultural transformation that he brought about in the USA would probably never have happened or would have been delayed for several years.

John Maynard Keynes was lucky to have been born in a family of scholars who could afford to take him to the best schools where he received a first-class education. Not only that. His primary area of study at university was mathematics. It is one of his professors, Alfred Marshall, who convinced him to pursue graduate studies in economics. If this event had not happened, then the world would probably not have benefitted from Keynesian economic theories.

The story of Christopher Columbus has unique elements of luck too. After intense lobbying, Columbus received sponsorship for his voyage to America from Queen Isabella I and King Ferdinand II. It is incredible to note that this sponsorship came almost as an afterthought. The monarchy was not sold on Columbus's proposal. They only offered to sponsor him to prevent the project from ending up in the hands of other rulers.

In almost all stories of the great people covered in this book, the element of luck is involved in one way or another. However, knowing the lucky or unlucky circumstances that contributed to somebody's greatness is not very helpful because luck is mostly beyond our control.

Having said that, I would conjecture that there are things that we can do in our individual lives that can enhance our propensity for good luck. The truth is that if we live a life of procrastination, then there is very little luck that will come our way. Conversely, if we remain active and continuously seek ways to better ourselves, we are likely to be better predisposed to good luck. I would argue that luck tends to favor those who are well prepared.

CHAPTER 17

A Tough Upbringing

There is no success without hardship.
- Sophocles

URING THE FEW TIMES THAT I have met my old friends from Naivasha Boarding School, the first topic of discussion has almost always been about our tough times at the school. The conversation would almost always invariably be with immense humor and a sense of appreciation for how life at Naivasha Boarding School toughened us to face challenges in our future lives.

By today's standards, Naivasha Boarding School was like a military barracks (the only difference being that we would go home for a one-month break at the end of every three months).

We would laugh about Njuguna Wazim, who was one class ahead of me. Njuguna occasionally performed some amusing antics as he tried to revolt against the hardships at school. There is a time when he was brought to school by his parents at the beginning of the term. His parents spent several hours in the school attending to school fees and other administrative issues.

The parents departed at around noon after bidding farewell to Njuguna Wazim. However, when they arrived at their home in Nakuru later in the evening, they were shocked to find Njuguna Wazim sitting comfortably on a sofa in the living room.

Njuguna Wazim had sneaked out of school just after his parents had bid him farewell. He had run to Naivasha town and taken the first bus to Nakuru.

The parents brought Njuguna Wazim back to school the following day. The headmaster dispensed several canes on his buttocks to teach him a lesson on the consequences of running away from school.

But the rod appeared to have had little impact. Running away from school became a habit for Njuguna Wazim, despite the automatic severe punishment when he was forcefully returned to the school by his parents. He calmed down after several school terms.

Another example that comes to mind vividly was that of Musandi (not his real name). Musandi reminds me of the quick psychological transformation that can happen to an individual when they find themselves in challenging circumstances.

Musandi was from a well-to-do family in Nairobi and joined the school around the middle of the school year. He wore spectacles, which was something that had never been seen before at Naivasha Boarding School.

He spoke with a well-polished English accent, something close to the American accent. He carried himself with an air of sophistication that created a certain distance between him and other ordinary students, most of whom were from small towns like Nakuru, Naivasha, and other far-flung villages.

In his first few days in school, only students with a high level of self-confidence could muster the courage to engage him in conversation. He was exceptional.

It was difficult to understand how someone of such high status than other students had landed at Naivasha Boarding School.

However, as the days passed by, the polish on Musandi started wearing away. This phenomenon was primarily attributable to the unsophisticated never-changing daily diet of porridge for breakfast; *ugali* (staple starch cornmeal made with maize flour) and cabbage for lunch; and boiled maize and beans for supper.

Additionally, Musandi found himself having to follow a strict school routine of rising up at 5:00 am to have a cold shower, followed by mandatory exercises in the field (during the cold season) and other exceptionally challenging routines. He also came face to face with ruthless teachers who did not tolerate unfinished homework or any other forms of tardiness.

Musandi was also swallowed up by another unique culture in the school. Life at Naivasha Boarding School was so tough that it had turned some students into muggers. Typically, when a parent or a relative visited a student, the relative would bring some goodies. The most common types of goodies were loaves of bread, *mandazi* (buns), and *chapatis*.

Some prefects in the school introduced a system whereby every student who was visited by a relative had to hand over to the prefects a portion of the goodies. The prefects called it customs duty. Over time, however, this habit deteriorated into a situation where the prefects were using extreme coercion to obtain a portion of the students' goodies. It became so bad that even other students who were not prefects joined in.

The incredible thing is that even the previously sophisticated Musandi became one of the muggers. On one particular occasion, he took the savagery to new levels that had never been seen at Naivasha Boarding School. He had just arrived at the scene where some students had just finished snatching bread from a student. There was nothing left to snatch. But not so for Musandi. In an act of barbaric desperation, Musandi caught one of the students by the neck forcefully snatched the bread from the student. A Nairobi sophisticate had mutated into a vicious mugger.

Whenever I think of Musandi, I think of how a normal human being can turn into a savage if placed under challenging conditions. Something strange seems to happen in a young person's psyche when they are subjected to harsh conditions. And the outcome can sometimes be horrifying, and in some cases, the result can tip the scales on the positive side.

We see examples of this type of behavioral transformation in the lives of some of the historical figures that we have covered in this book. A tough upbringing can, indeed, create exceptional individuals.

Toughened by Early Childhood Conditions

STARTING WITH MALCOLM X ONCE AGAIN, we see an individual who experienced extreme racial hatred when he was a young boy. White supremacists torched the house that he called home. His father, Reverend Earl Little, was run over by a streetcar on September 28, 1931, and died later in hospital. The white supremacist group, the Black Legion, allegedly orchestrated the accident. His school teachers demeaned him too.

It is not hard to imagine what went through the mind of young Malcolm Little. His mind must have become filled with a toxic mixture of anger, frustration, and possibly a desire for vengeance. Therefore, it is not difficult to understand his transition to political activism when he became a young adult. And he was relentless and unapologetic in his quest for justice.

Martin Luther King Jr. and Nelson Mandela, the other influential political activists of the 20th century, went through different childhood experiences. They both came from reasonably decent family backgrounds. What appears to have sowed the seeds of activism in them was empathy for their fellow black people's suffering - the kind of suffering that Malcolm X experienced first-hand. The feelings of empathy must have mutated into such intense rage that Nelson Mandela was willing to die in pursuit of justice for the South African people. Martin Luther King Jr. too took significant risks too in the quest for freedom and equality for black Americans.

Another example is William the Conqueror. He was an illegitimate child, and some people were hell-bent on sticking that label on his young mind. They called him "William the Bastard."

Despite the shortcoming as an illegitimate child, William was thrust into the throne as Duke of Normandy at only eight years. It was not easy for him. People who were jostling for power even made an abortive attempt to kill him. Fortunately, he managed to escape to France in 1064, where he stayed under the protection of King of France, King Henry I.

What a cruel world that William had found himself in! Once again, it is not hard to imagine what went through his mind as he experienced these challenges. Thoughts of vengeance must have preoccupied him. And sure enough, in later years, he did live to exact his revenge ferociously.

We see the same type of hardship in Temujin's early life, who later changed his name to Genghis Khan.[56] Temujin witnessed the death of his father through poisoning by local tribesmen. This event happened suddenly. According to the tradition in Mongolia at that time, he was supposed to take over the position of clan chief from his father, but his fellow Borjigin tribesmen would not let him. The tribesmen refused to recognize him as their chief. They abandoned him. He ended up living a life full of hardship in a region of the world where violence was the order of the day.

But what perhaps scarred Temujin's mind forever was the raid of his village by warriors from the Merkit tribe when he was about 16, during which the raiders killed several people and also kidnapped his wife, Borte. It was a terrible experience.

Temujin did not let the matter end there. He planned for a counter-attack. The planning was exceptionally meticulous. Suffice it to say that the viciousness and brutality of Temujin's counter-attack could only be surpassed by the hurt that he had suffered earlier following the abduction of his wife, Borte.

The extent of Temujin's (Genghis Khan's) brutality in subsequent years was legendary. Some even refer to him as a "madman." The world was paying for its sins for hurting Temujin when he was growing up. One of the famous quotes attributed to him goes as follows: "I am the punishment of God...If you had not committed great sins, God would not have sent a punishment like me upon you."[57]

Beethoven, who grew into one of the best musicians that the world has ever seen, went through a tough childhood too. He suffered beatings from his alcoholic father and even suffered the mental anguish of watching his father beat his mother. He survived the harshness and went on to become an accomplished musician.

John Lennon, the other famous musician, lived a strange dysfunctional life as a young boy, initially under the care of his mother and an absentee father. His mother got a child with another man and left John Lennon to be raised by relatives. It was not a wonder that John Lennon performed poorly in high school. However, when he learned how to play the guitar, he did not look back. His angels steered him in a musical direction that was to lead him to a tremendously successful career in the music industry.

One of the earliest and most impressive philosophers, Aristotle, also led an unusual life in early childhood. He lost his parents when he was 13 and was brought up by guardians.

Abraham Lincoln, too, underwent a lot of hardship when he was growing up. His mother died when he was nine years old. He was brought up by his 11-year old sister. His father subjected him to hard labor on the farm. Abraham Lincoln ended up hating farming. His father also subjected him to beatings. Some historians have suggested that the cruel treatment by his father reminded Abraham Lincoln of the harsh treatment of slaves. When Abraham Lincoln became president of the United States of America, one of his first legislative accomplishments was to abolish slavery.

Another unusual leader in the Genghis Khan league was Adolf Hitler. Many people remember Hitler for the untold death and destruction that he caused in Europe. Perhaps his harsh life as he was growing up was partly to blame.

Adolf Hitler was born in a relatively low-income family. He does not appear to have enjoyed the necessities of an average child growing up in Austria. He became an anti-social individual. He frequently had issues with his father. And similar to Beethoven, he also received beatings from his father. Hitler dropped out of high school.

When Hitler applied to join the Art school in Vienna, he was rejected, not once, but twice. He lived a life of struggles in Vienna in his teen years. Sometimes he did casual jobs to survive.

Hitler grew into an angry individual who meted vengeance against society in the most horrible way imaginable. The irony is that, in his early years as the leader of Germany, he initiated transformative projects that would have propelled Germany to great heights were it not for his subsequent greed and utter brutality.

These few examples suggest that the kind of life that people go through when they are children plays a significant role in shaping their characters in later life. And, as we have seen, individuals who go through a harsh upbringing sometimes grow up into exceptional individuals who may do things that tip the scales in terms of positivity or negativity.

SO, WHAT DOES THIS TELL us in terms of how we should nurture youngsters?

I hypothesize that it would pay dividends, in the long-term, to innovate in programs aimed at toughening up our youngsters. I am not advocating for the harsh, cruel treatment similar to what people like Beethoven went through. That kind of treatment is likely to create monsters like Hitler.

I am thinking of programs such as beefing up and expanding boy scouts and girl guides associations; and, most importantly, introducing activities that would genuinely teach courage, bravery, and independent-mindedness of the youngsters. In other words, substantially increasing investment in programs aimed at molding individuals into strong characters.

CHAPTER 18

The Role of Education

The great aim of education is not knowledge but action.

— Herbert Spencer

I HAVE PERSONALLY NOT SEEN ANYTHING that is as transformative in an individual's life as education. That is probably why parents in Kenya, and no doubt in other parts of the world, make significant personal sacrifices in the quest for a good education for their children.

When I look at the life paths of my school mates from Naivasha Boarding School, there is a close correlation between their level of success in life and their education.

Firstly, good performance at Naivasha Boarding School meant that a student would be admitted into a good high school. Entry into a good high school increased a student's chances of good performance at high school and subsequently getting admission into an institution of higher learning. And entry into an institution of higher education made the most significant difference in one's career path and standard of living as an adult.

Things have changed in the past few years as the country's population has grown, and job opportunities have become increasingly competitive. But one fact is clear in my mind. Those with a good education stand a far better chance than those without a good education.

However, in terms of achieving greatness, the picture is not so clear-cut when we examine the lives of the historical greats covered in this book.

The Role of Education

EDUCATION SEEMS TO PLAY AN essential part in laying the foundation for greatness, but there are exceptions.

Starting with Malcolm X once again, we see education playing a significant role in his life. This assertion may seem contradictory when you consider that Malcolm X was a school dropout. However, if you look closer, you will see something quite extraordinary.

Malcolm X dropped out of school partly because one of his teachers told him that he would never achieve his ambition of becoming a lawyer —an exceptionally insensitive way for a teacher to talk to a pupil.

After dropping out of school and going to the city, it was not long before Malcolm X got into trouble with the authorities. But it is what happened later while he was in prison that is truly inspiring.

Malcolm X could hardly read or write when he went to jail. Still, he gradually developed a considerable desire for learning. He started by teaching himself how to read and write by going through a dictionary meticulously, from the letter A to the letter Z. Over time, this activity enabled him to become fully literate.

When Malcolm X became literate, he started reading voraciously. He read anything that he could find in the prison library. His interest in reading was so great that there are times when he used the dim light coming through the crevices of his jail cell to continue reading late at night after the guards had switched off the lights in the cells.[58]

The story of Malcolm X's initiation into education while in prison should be essential reading for everyone who wishes to pursue a career in adult education.

For Martin Luther King and Nelson Mandela, on the other hand, education was at the core of who they were. Martin Luther King pursued education to the highest level, earning a Ph.D. in theology at Boston University. Mandela studied and graduated in law before he became fully engrossed in political activism. It is fair to conclude that their thinking to start agitating for freedom and justice for their people emerged from insights that they gained from their education.

John Maynard Keynes, whose ideas in economics revolutionized economic management in many nations, had a sound educational background. He was lucky to have been born in a family that valued education. His father was an administrator and a lecturer at one of the most prestigious universities in the world, Cambridge University.

Aristotle, the great ancient philosopher, was one of the inventors of formal education. Any discussion of education would be incomplete without the mention of Aristotle and his enormous contribution to human knowledge.

In more recent years, we saw the example of Karl Marx, who obtained an excellent education, firstly through private tuition until age 12 from his father, who was a lawyer, followed by a transition to university to study law and philosophy. Although he was a problematic student, he eventually graduated from the university, after which he started writing extensively. The volume of material that he wrote was mind-boggling.

The story of Abraham Lincoln's self-education is quite incredible. He did not follow the conventional path in education, but he eventually qualified as a lawyer. One can narrate the story of Abraham Lincoln in terms of how a young man who was born in a log cabin on Sinking Spring Farm,

Kentucky, became hungry for education. And through sheer determination, he lifted himself with his bootstraps to pursue an educational goal that he ultimately achieved. An education that provided him a solid foundation for an exceptionally successful career in politics.

Mikhail Gorbachev is another excellent example of the power of education. He was a brilliant student from a very young age. He studied in one of the most prestigious universities in the Soviet Union (he met his wife, a Ph. D. scholar at the university). He obtained two university degrees, which paved the way for his career in politics.

For the scientists Isaac Newton, Leonhard Euler, and Albert Einstein, education was at the core of what they did and the fame that followed. However, the fascinating part of it is that none of these individuals was considered exceptionally bright when going through the school system. And yet, they made such significant accomplishments in human knowledge, an important fact that should be at the top of every young scientist's mind today.

These examples suggest that education is vital towards creating individuals with the capacity to propel humanity to high levels.

On the other hand, it is quite amazing to note that numerous other individuals who had an enormous influence on the world did not benefit from formal education. A good example is Michelangelo. He hated schooling but had a passion for art, a calling considered inferior to other professions at the time. Interestingly, despite his enormous talent in painting, he preferred to think of himself as a sculptor - an art form in which he had great talent.

The other example is Picasso, who grew up in a reasonably decent middle-class family but did not get much formal education. But this drawback notwithstanding, he went on to become one of the best artists that the world has ever seen. He was born with a natural talent for art.

Looking at the example of Michelangelo and Picasso, one may be tempted to conclude that when it comes to matters of art, what counts is a natural talent. But is that all that made these individuals great? We will explore this question a little later.

How about in business? Henry Ford, who transformed millions of lives in America in the late 1800 and early 1900, was a school drop-out.

When I first read the story of Henry Ford, I was so entranced by it. I could not reconcile in my mind, for several days, how one individual could have such a significant impact on society. Other individuals did equally big things in the business world in later years. Still, Henry Ford stands out for revolutionizing the business landscape and significantly changing peoples' culture. And yet, he did not have any formal education to write home about. So, there must have been something else about him that contributed to his greatness. We will come back to this shortly too.

Another enigmatic individual was Christopher Columbus, who opened up the western world. And yet, he did not have any formal schooling either. His education was self-taught. He would not have even contemplated going on a risky expedition by sea if he was not confident about his knowledge of navigation. But was this, presumably modest, self-taught education, what made him great? There must have been something else.

There is not much that historians know about the education of Vasco Da Gama, another brave explorer. Still, he too etched his name in history by exploring East Asia, despite his limited formal education.

But perhaps the most exceptional example is William Shakespeare. He did not have much of an education when he was young, mainly due to issues of school fees. He dropped out of school when he was just 13. Still, it is incredible that William Shakespeare is studied in English literature classes in many universities across the world.

Percy Bysshe Shelley, another literary giant, although brought up in an upper-class family, and taken to one of the most prestigious universities in the world, Oxford, did not graduate. He did not graduate due to misbehavior. He subsequently lived a strange life full of intrigue. And yet, he is considered one of the great English poets.

William the Conqueror was born in a monarchy. He was thrust into power as a Duke before he was even a teenager. There is no evidence of his formal education, and yet he grew into one of the most notable rulers in the United Kingdom. The symbols of his reign are visible in the United Kingdom up to this day. For example, the Tower of London, which he commissioned in 1066.

It is noteworthy that some people think of William the Conqueror as one of the most vicious tyrants that ever-ruled England.

Another example is Genghis Khan. He does not appear to have had a formal education either. Still, his impact on world affairs reverberates up to this day. It is interesting to note that one hardly hears the word Mongolia mentioned in the mass media today, and yet the people of Mongolia, led initially by Genghis Khan, were at one time on the verge of creating a world empire.

"Come again, the Mongols? Those blood-thirsty brutish sods so close to animals that we named a major genetic deficiency after them?" asks Aldo Matteucci.[59]

Consider Mozart, too, one of the most prolific music composers of the Classical period. The only formal education that he received was the music that his father taught him. He was a musical genius. But, once again, the big question is whether his transformation into a great musician was attributable solely to his talent in music.

John Lennon, a musical genius of the modern era, had an unfortunate upbringing with his parents breaking up when he was just five years old. His relatives raised him. He did not seem to have much interest in schooling. He was a friendly character but was not serious about his studies. His biography states that his typical school report had unpleasant comments from his teachers, such as "Certainly on the road to failure ... hopeless ... rather a clown in class ... wasting other pupils' time."[60]

Yet, John Lennon became a pop music icon of the 1960s, thanks to his exceptional talent in playing the guitar. So, there was something more than education to his success.

Jean Jacques Rousseau, a man whose philosophical writings, particularly his book *Social Contract*, inspired the French Revolution and revolutions in other parts of the world, did not have any formal schooling. In his autobiography, he stated that he received a haphazard education from his father until the age of ten.[61]

Sometime between 1728 and 1731, Jean Jacques Rousseau trained briefly to become a priest. He switched to a career as an itinerant musician and teacher. Interestingly, his writings on the education of children, particularly his treatise *Emile*, are cited by educational scholars up to this day. And this is the work of someone who did not go to university.

Adolf Hitler stormed the world stage and committed horrendous acts against humanity. He was a school dropout. People talk about his actions with anger and disdain. Could he have done the horrible things because of his lack of education? The answer to that question is a matter of conjecture.

And then there was Muhammad Ali, a native of Kentucky, in the USA, who did not go beyond high school and entered into the boxing world almost by accident. And yet he became one of the most famous and influential boxers of all time.

So, based on the examples described above, one must wonder whether something else, beyond education, is responsible for the phenomenon of greatness. True, a tough upbringing helps, and so does education, but surely there must be something else.

CHAPTER 19

Good Character Traits

Character is one of the greatest motive powers in the world. In its noblest embodiments, it exemplifies human nature in its highest forms, for it exhibits man at his best.

– Samuel Smiles.

WHEN TEACHERS AT NAIVASHA BOARDING School selected the student leadership body; they seemed to choose those who had certain character traits. Typically, prefects would be students who performed well in class, or students who did well in sports, or were exceptionally well behaved.

Some students just seemed to be naturally endowed with these qualities, perhaps by virtue of how they had been brought up by their parents or the environment in which they had grown. For example, individuals who came from ethnic backgrounds where there was a clear path from childhood through adulthood, with different initiation stages into the various levels in the social strata, seemed to have a particular inbuilt self-confidence that served them well.

The students from the urban centers, on the other hand, seemed to be at a disadvantage. But over time, such students matured into well-rounded individuals.

Looking at the historical figures covered in this book, we see certain common character traits among many individuals. The big question is whether these character traits turned them into the great legends they became.

SOME OF THE COMMON CHARACTER traits that we see when we look at the great political activists Malcolm X, Martin Luther King Jr., and Nelson Mandela are perseverance, courage, relentlessness, and a clear vision.

In the case of the great artists Michelangelo and Picasso, we see a tremendous passion, stubbornness, and a constant search for excellence. They were also individuals who were relentless in their pursuits.

In Henry Ford, we see an individual who possessed fierce determination, passion, perseverance, audacity, relentlessness, innovativeness, stubbornness, and a monomaniacal focus on details. He was also courageous and immensely action-orientation.

John Maynard Keynes achieved greatness through the power of his intellect, being unconventional, and having the courage to hold an opinion contrary to the prevailing wisdom. He was a free-thinking individual who was not afraid of rocking the boat in pursuit of putting his ideas into action.

The explorer Christopher Columbus was characteristic of his relentlessness, courage, and quest for adventure. He maintained a sharp focus on his objective and sought sponsorship persistently, despite constant rejection. His fellow adventurer, Vasco da Gama, showed similar character traits of relentlessness, courage, and being adventurous, a sharp focus on his objectives, and persistence towards achieving his goals.

In English literature, we meet an exceptional individual, William Shakespeare. A person with an extraordinary literary talent, a talent that could only be matched by his immense determination, passion, perseverance, and courage in the face of adversity. He was also stubborn and relentless in his literary pursuits. In Percy Bysshe Shelley, we see an unconventional, idealistic, and uncompromising individual; who was radical and possessed a unique determination to put his ideas into action despite the attendant risks.

In our exploration of the great monarchical leaders, we see tremendous bravery in Ramesses, matched with extraordinary skills in public administration. In William the Conqueror, we see a courageous leader, a strategic thinker, and an exceptionally meticulous planner.

On the other hand, Genghis Khan was in a class of his own in terms of display of unconditional love, courage, and big thinking. The character trait that he shared with other monarchs, and more so with William the Conqueror, was a heightened sense of vengeance and unmatched brutality in pursuit of retribution.

In Mozart and Beethoven, we see the exceptional musical genius that they enhanced through passion, hard work, and partly through the mentorship and coaching from others. John Lennon is an example of someone with great ambition and drive, and a hard worker who was also predisposed to combining work with fun.

Aristotle was a philosopher of unmatched talents. He valued education immensely, was independent-minded, and promoted clear, logical reasoning. He also had excellent influencing skills.

Jean Jacques Rousseau was equally independent-minded and instigated action through the power of his great intellect. Karl Marx was another philosopher in a class of his own. He possessed an unsurpassed love for education and conducted extensive research. And perhaps most of all, he was immensely action-oriented.

HISTORICAL SNAPSHOTS OF THE GREAT

In politics, we see Abraham Lincoln, another hardworking individual who lifted himself with his bootstraps to reach the highest political office in the USA. He was a schemer and highly action-oriented.

Adolf Hitler, on the other hand, was an unusual character. He thrived in propaganda games, was uncompromising, and highly manipulative. This character trait caused tremendous harm to the world. In Mikhail Gorbachev, we see another individual who valued education, was hard-working, and action-oriented too.

In the religious leaders, Jesus Christ, Muhammad, and Sri Krishna, we see faith, love, forgiveness, virtue, and humility. We also see kindness and a deep sense of self-realization.

In Isaac Newton, Leonhard Euler, and Albert Einstein, we see examples of exceptional genius, hard work, and innovation. And in all three cases, we see individuals who are not willing to just flow along with the status quo.

Muhammad Ali exemplifies success achieved through determination, hard work, tremendous self-confidence, and a strong belief in intensive training.

And in the case of writers, we see Leo Tolstoy, a literary genius who worked tirelessly to generate enormous amounts of literature. Ernest Hemingway was another eccentric character whose success was driven by his unique talent as a writer and a knack for shunning the status quo.

All the character traits described above played a significant role in making the individuals covered in this book hugely influential. And with a few exceptions, the character traits are worth emulating to achieve personal success. Many people already possess some of the character traits described above. But, what do they need to do to achieve the kind of phenomenal influence that the individuals covered in this book accomplished? I submit that this is a question that we can only answer individually based on our intimate knowledge of personal limitations and strengths.

Indeed, most of the self-help literature that one finds in libraries and book stores focuses on different techniques of building these character traits as a prerequisite for success in life. The young generation can benefit immensely by adopting these character traits (except the few negative, destructive character ones).

CHAPTER 20

Being Proactive

*Wouldn't it be ironic if everyone who got a radio up
and running just sat around waiting for everyone else
to transmit a message?*
— Patricia Hamill

THE ONE COMMON DENOMINATOR THAT I see in almost all of the great influencers covered in this book, in different degrees, is "**proactiveness.**" It does not matter what circumstances that they were born in or the kind of upbringing that they received; what they all seem to have in common is "proactiveness." In other words, the ability to take action to control a situation or events rather than responding to external stimuli and the capacity to take action to pursue a particular goal with immense zeal.

If you consider the activists Malcolm X, Martin Luther King, and Nelson Mandela, for example, you will see that these are individuals who saw injustice happening in society and decided to take action rather than just take a back seat and watch. They took action despite the immense risks to their personal lives. And not only that, after they had decided to take action, they pursued their goals relentlessly.

The activists recruited followers to help them in their journey of seeking justice for their fellow citizens. Other people joined them too, without being prompted, because they could identify with the courses that the three individuals were pursuing. The proactiveness of the three activists created a certain aura that naturally caused people to gravitate towards them.

Michelangelo and Picasso had unparalleled natural talents in art. Still, it was their proactiveness that propelled them into the pinnacle of the art world. We can see streaks of this proactiveness in their careers.

When Michelangelo became a sculpturing apprentice in Bertoldo di Giovani's workshop, other apprentices became jealous of his superior sculpturing skills. They tried to frustrate him so that he could quit. Still, Michelangelo stood his ground firmly, occasionally getting involved in fistfights with them.

Michelangelo then sought work proactively in Rome, speaking directly to the Cardinal there to get commissions. The immensely beautiful works that he produced for the Cardinal have stood the test of time and are a significant tourist attraction in Rome up to this day.

We see similar streaks of proactiveness in Pablo Picasso. However, the one that struck me the most was his decision to transition from classical paintings to cubism. All business leaders should study this phase of Picasso's life to get insights on strategy in the face of a significant change looming on the horizon.

Picasso, sensing the dramatic effect that photography would have on art, decided to take a bold, proactive action that puzzled even his colleagues in the art community.

Previously, paintings of landscapes and individuals were the primary sources of revenue for artists. However, photography that had just been invented was capable of capturing the images of landscapes and people with precise accuracy rendering the work of the artists almost irrelevant. But not so for Picasso. He invented cubism, a form of abstract art that was aesthetically fascinating, albeit initially shocking to others in the art community.

Cubism steered Picasso into the pinnacle of the art world. His actions were a demonstration of tremendous foresight and proactiveness. He benefited immensely from his proactiveness, and so did the world in general.

If I were to rank the great leaders covered in this book according to their proactiveness, then Henry Ford would be right at the top of my list. Scholars in business schools discuss his proactive business decisions up to this day.

Henry Ford did not have a university degree. He used the engineering knowledge he gained as an apprentice in machining workshops in Detroit to build an automobile. This activity caused a rift between him and his employer, the Detroit Edison Company. Henry Ford was, however, not deterred. He looked for financial backers who helped him set up his own automobile company, the Ford Motor Company.

Henry Ford also went out of his way to perfect automobile production techniques. And when his business started growing, he did what many people would perhaps not have imagined at the time. He acquired a vast piece of land (2,000-acres) near River Rouge and built on it what would become the largest car manufacturing plant in the world.

It took about ten years to build the River Rouge factory. And when the factory was ready, it started churning out cars in the thousands, making the Ford Motor Company one of the largest car manufacturers in the world.

Although other problems subsequently beset Henry Ford, he made an indelible mark in the history of business in the world. And at the heart of it was his disposition to thinking big and always taking proactive action to grow the business bigger and bigger.

John Maynard Keynes is undoubtedly one of the historical greats who were well-grounded in a good solid education. But unlike many scholars of his time, he did not merely adhere to the status quo. He was brave enough to take a different path when he was convinced that everybody else was moving in the wrong direction. For example, after the end of the First World War when everyone was literally at the throat of the Germans and wanted them to pay the highest price in war reparations, Maynard Keynes, who was a member of the British delegation that was negotiating the Treaty of Versailles, walked out of the conference. He argued that the allied forces had taken the wrong approach by making excessive demands on the Germans. His view was that such unreasonable demands would not only destroy the German economy, making it difficult for the Germans to pay for the war reparations, it would also sow the seeds of resentment, with potentially negative repercussions in later years. Maynard Keynes was later proved right with the emergence of Adolf Hitler in Germany a few years later.

Also, Maynard Keynes did not believe in the effectiveness of classical economic theories promulgated by the likes of Adam Smith, who believed in the free market economy. Keynes believed that during times of economic recession, the proactive action of the government was essential to revitalizing an economy, rather than the government merely taking a back seat and letting market forces bring about the necessary equilibrium.

Maynard Keynes proactively sold his ideas to the British and other governments, triggering economic policies across different parts of the world that benefited millions of people.

If Maynard Keynes had held onto his ideas without going out of his way to convince government policymakers to put the ideas into action, we would probably be living in a very different world today, a world that would perhaps be less prosperous.

The explorer, Christopher Columbus, exemplifies the notion of proactiveness in a different way. A closer look at his biography reveals that his desire to go on a voyage to discover new lands was motivated to a considerable extent by a quest for glory and material riches. But even if that was the case, he took exemplary proactive action to make it happen.

Christopher Columbus lobbied extensively for support. He was turned down several times, but that did not dampen his spirits. He continued searching for sponsors relentlessly. Eventually, the tide turned in his favor. He received the backing that he was looking for and finally set sail to look for a new route to Asia through the Atlantic Ocean.

Christopher Columbus met with multiple obstacles along the way, including a small mutiny inside his vessel from sailors who had become tired and wanted to return to Spain as the voyage seemed headed nowhere. But he was unfazed. He did his best to convince the sailors to remain hopeful and press on with the journey. The perseverance eventually yielded positive results.

A similar kind of proactiveness and determination to pursue a path that had not been tried before can also be seen in Vasco da Gama.

Turning to the famous literary figures, we see different aspects of proactiveness too. Despite having a limited educational background, William Shakespeare did not just remain at his home village of Stratford-upon-Avon. He made the significant step of moving to London. He joined the theatre community and took the tremendous initiative of writing plays that were performed in the theatre there.

And when the landlords brought down the theatre for profitability reasons, Shakespeare did not retreat in despair. He took proactive action to re-create the theatre in a different location in London, despite his meager resources. The new theatre lacked certain physical elements, but Shakespeare made good for the shortfall through his creative writing, achieving great success.

Percy Bysshe Shelley is probably remembered not because of his dysfunctional love affairs but for his literary works, which he deliberately used to instigate action. A different writer would probably have just written his literature and left it at that. But Percy Bysshe Shelley was different. He wanted to go one step further, proactively instigating action through his written works. It was a dangerous thing to do and probably cost him his life in the end.

Survival in the ancient monarchical systems would not have been possible without constant proactive action by those in power. It was a vicious world. Ramesses the Great, for example, is remembered for the battles he fought as he proactively tried to regain territory taken away from Egypt.

The Battle of Hastings, for which William the Conqueror is arguably most famous, was a deliberate adventure to take power from Harold. William the Conqueror believed that Harold had wrongly assumed the crown after the death of Edward the Confessor, the King of England.

The proactive measures that William the Conqueror took to secure his power base and ensure effective administration of the Kingdom were unprecedented, including the unparalleled census of people and property in England.

Genghis Khan became one of the most successful leaders in history by putting together a disciplined military force to go after his enemies. And when he had finished meting out justice on the enemies, he took proactive action to conquer territories adjoining his Kingdom of Mongolia. He went even further to other distant lands to preempt future attacks and plunder on behalf of his Mongolian people, albeit the morality of the latter initiative was questionable.

HISTORICAL SNAPSHOTS OF THE GREAT

One could argue that Mozart became a renowned musician due to his father's efforts in arranging for Mozart's performances in different places in Europe. To that extent, one could say that the proactive action of his father, Leopold Mozart, is what made Mozart successful and famous.

The Beethoven phenomenon, too, was mainly the product of an overbearing and strict father who was hell-bent on making Beethoven into a great musician. And he succeeded.

The case of John Lennon, however, is different. He was mostly self-made. But it is quite surprising that after a poor showing in academics in primary and secondary school, he decided to set up a band when he was just 15. That band would end up becoming the vehicle that would steer his musical career to exceptional heights.

I would argue that it is almost impossible to become a successful philosopher without a proactive mindset. Nobody exemplifies this notion more than Aristotle. Here was someone who created new vistas of knowledge through proactive intellectual inquiry in many fields, from physics to biology.

The Jean Jacques phenomenon is, at its core, a study in proactive action. Rousseau not only wrote great philosophy, but his ideas triggered political action in France and other parts of the world. He was a believer in proactive action to gain political freedom.

Karl Marx was in a class of his own. I would put him very high on the list of proactive historical figures. His ideas on Marxism were cookbooks on how to proactively overthrow the status quo, a status that he believed was unfair to the working class. And he used his humongous intellect to propagate ideas that shook the world. His ideas are still applied by different people in different parts of the world today. But his most distinct attribute was the lengths to which he went to propagate his ideas.

Politicians, like the monarchy, would not survive without being proactive. Abraham Lincoln's life has multiple examples of an exceptionally proactive individual. He did not go through the formal education system smoothly, but this did not deter him. He took proactive action to obtain an education and eventually qualified as a lawyer. He took proactive action to lift his profile within the court system, and ultimately within the Republican Party. At the time of the Presidential elections in 1860, he had proved himself. He earned the confidence of other politicians in the Republican party. Accordingly, his nomination to vie for the presidency came easily.

Abraham Lincoln's time in office was marked with different proactive actions. He led his administration to defeat the Confederate forces. He also successfully introduced legislation prohibiting slavery, a practice that he abhorred since his days as a boy working on his father's farm in Kentucky.

Adolf Hitler's story is familiar to many people. But perhaps the interesting part is how he grew from an uneducated political underdog into an influential political figure, a feat that he accomplished through different types of political machinations.

Michael Gorbachev, too, was a relatively young party lieutenant when he got into politics. But his story shows just how aggressive he was in his quest to climb the ladder in the political establishment. His strong educational credentials served him well. And perhaps more notably, he introduced *perestroika* and *glasnost*, two novel economic management approaches that caught many Russians by surprise.

Some historians have attributed the collapse of the Soviet Union to *perestroika* and *glasnost*. Still, many people believe that Gorbachev ushered in democracy in the Soviet Union, which earned him a Nobel Prize. In essence, it was a prize for proactiveness in the face of an oppressive and failing political system.

Based on the discoveries and innovations that they are credited for, Isaac Newton, Leonhard Euler, and Albert Einstein are perhaps the best examples of proactiveness in science and technology. Without being proactive in looking behind existing knowledge and daring to develop new ideas, they would not have achieved the kind of fame that they enjoy in the scientific community today.

In sports, too, being proactive has its rewards. Muhammad Ali demonstrated this with his famous taunts of his opponents that weakened the opponents psychologically before major fights. And more importantly, Ali's open demonstration of personal aggrandizement made him a darling of the mass media. He earned immense free publicity from these public relations stunts deliberately aimed at creating hype in the boxing world. He did it with style and succeeded enormously, making boxing one of the most popular and entertaining sports in the world for decades.

Leo Tolstoy provides us with yet another perspective of proactiveness. He did not just let life pass by unrecorded. He maintained a diary of his daily activities. This diary later helped him create some of the most passionate and inspirational literature that has ever come from Russia.

On the other hand, Ernest Hemingway was a troublesome student in high school but excelled in English. He used this strength to go into a career where he felt comfortable. He started in journalism, where he honed his writing skills to become one of America's best writers ever. He made his mark by taking a new writing style that he learned at the Kansas City Star to new literary heights, endearing himself to many readers, and earning two prestigious prizes, the Pulitzer Prize and the Nobel Prize for Literature.

So, **proactiveness** seems to be the critical defining attribute of great people.

A Call to Action

We need to teach our children, our youngsters, and everyone else in society how to adopt a proactive mindset, irrespective of their calling.

Proactiveness in Action

FOR PROACTIVENESS TO BE MOST effective, one must have a clear sense of direction. The question that then arises is: how does one develop a meaningful sense of direction?

There is no simple answer to this question because people are different and have different motivations in life.

However, as a starting point, we can state anecdotally that most people feel satisfied with their current situation. Perhaps, this is the insight that the Irish poet and playwright, Oscar Wilde, intended to convey, albeit from a slightly different angle when he said that "the world belongs to the discontented."[62]

Indeed, the lack of contentment is a notion that is at the core of the theory of philosophy called existentialism. The theory falls under the branch of philosophy called metaphysics discussed in chapter 9.

One of the scholars associated with existentialism theory was the Nobel Laureate, Jean-Paul Sartre, who averred that we live in an absurd universe where we are continually trying to look for the meaning of life. Further, our anxiety stems from our uncertain existence and the responsibility associated with the limitless choice and freedom that we possess.[63]

For our present purposes, we could say that discontentment is also partly a manifestation of the lack of fulfillment of our desired goals.

The lack of fulfillment could be perceived as a continuum of discontent, with different people falling on various points along that continuum.

Some are discontent because they have not found a suitable path to their desired destination. Others are still on a journey towards an unfulfilled goal, while others may have veered off course and are unsure of meeting their goal. And there are multiple other variations of triggers of dissatisfaction along the continuum of discontent.

Many people may feel that they are victims of circumstances and have very little room for maneuver. One could argue that this is the kind of mindset that holds people back, the sort of malady that ought to be cured by proactiveness.

Being proactive means evaluating one's current position, determining where one wants to go despite one's current circumstances, and making the mental leap to break away from the shackles of the status quo. Taking positive actions to move towards one's desired destination.

In other words, rather than lingering in the existential anxiety and dread described by Jean-Paul Sartre, one should unshackle their mind from that situation and leap into the promising future by leveraging the limitless choice and freedom that one possesses.

Dwelling too much on the historical factors that have brought one to their present circumstances may be an exercise in futility because one cannot change history. It is like someone with a phobia for heights looking down after climbing a few steps on a ladder. Looking down only creates vertigo and prevents one from proceeding with their upward ascent to greater heights.

Proactiveness means taking action without prompting. One should also avoid the temptation of waiting for cues from others before taking bold action into the unknown. Proactiveness means building the mental capacity to take a step towards one's desired destination without necessarily waiting for permission from others.

But a proactive mindset needs to be rooted in a solid ethical foundation, rooted in one's cultural context. It would be counter-productive to vigorously pursue a particular goal if one ends up causing unnecessary harm to others. A solid moral foundation is essential to assist one in making the right decisions along the way.

However, having a strong ethical foundation does not mean fear of raffling some feathers along the way. We live in an exceptionally competitive world. The chances are that the journey to success will likely be littered with traps and obstacles deliberately placed by others to hinder one's progress. It is also a journey that may be fraught with jealousy and resentment from others. One should remain proactively focused on their goal and ignore or jump over the obstacles. Many a time, the barriers will, in any event, be shadows of monsters that can be frightening but are harmless.

When one is on their journey towards their goal, one is likely to meet those who will try to feed their thoughts with negative ideas, innocently or otherwise, out of fear of the unknown. One should avoid such naysayers too.

Importantly, proactiveness means freedom from procrastination. It means taking action "now."

If you want to be a good cook and bought some cookery books some time back, books you have not yet touched, ask yourself: "What am I waiting for?" If you cannot find a watertight answer to this question, walk to your bookshelf and pick the books. Start reading them today. Plan to finish them in a reasonable time. Also, go into the kitchen later today and start trying out the new recipes.

If you have been thinking of becoming an actor, but nothing is happening, ask yourself: "What am I waiting for?" If there is nothing you are waiting for, pick up the phone, or start browsing the internet to identify suitable leads. And do not stop there; once you identify the leads, then start making the necessary calls.

If you genuinely want to excel as a student, then you most probably know precisely the amount of effort that you need to put into your studies to improve your grades. So, what are you waiting for? Go to your study now, and start becoming a good student.

If you want to write a book, take a pen and a piece of paper right now, and start writing. If you stare at the paper for five minutes without writing anything, ask yourself, "What am I waiting for?"

Continually asking yourself, "What am I waiting for?" will help slay the demons of procrastination.

Being proactive also requires one to be courageous. As William Shakespeare said:

A coward dies a thousand times before his death, but the valiant taste of death but once. It seems to me most strange that men should fear, seeing that death, a necessary end, will come when it will come.[64]

Courage is an essential ingredient of proactiveness. Many a time being proactive means leaping into the unknown. The rewards of making such a leap could be enormous.

Still, proactiveness also means being realistic about the potential for being disappointed. The vital point to bear in mind here is that if you let the fear of leaping overcome you, you will never know what you missed. Disappointment may strengthen you and point you in another direction that could potentially be even more fulfilling.

Being proactive means making a personal commitment to invest in the time and resources to propel you to your goal. If you have a job that is not paying well but need to get a higher qualification to get the kind of job you desire, ask yourself: "What am I waiting for?" If the answer to the question is feeble, then find out what it would take for you to get the qualification in terms of time and money. After obtaining the information, choose one or more steps to take today towards getting the qualification. Perhaps you will start a new routine of waking up at 5:00 am to study before you go to work. Just start doing something about it today.

If your family is falling apart because of something that you did or that was done to you some time back, and you are keen to start repairing the broken fences but have not started doing it, ask yourself: "What am I waiting for?" If you cannot find a good answer, then begin mending your fences right now, not tomorrow. It could be just a matter of a simple telephone call to say: "I apologize," or to say: "Can we meet tomorrow to talk it over?"

If you are a religious person aspiring to grow your spirituality, ask yourself: "What am I waiting for?" If you cannot find the right answer, then you most probably know what to do to grow spiritually. Do not look over your shoulders to see who is looking at you. Your actions are between you and your God. Just do what you believe is right, today, not tomorrow.

Where I come from, there is an old saying that goes as follows: "*Riua ritietagigira muthamaki.*" The translation of this saying is: "The sun does not wait for the King." In order words, the passage of time does not wait even for the King, no matter how powerful he may be. This adage is true of every mortal on this earth too. The few minutes that I have taken to write this sentence have vanished. I will never get that time ever again. So, one should never waste valuable time waiting. The golden question that one should always ask is: "What am I waiting for?"

In summary, the critical ingredients of proactiveness are deciding what one wants to achieve in life and taking action to propel oneself towards that goal.

Proactiveness requires one to take action without prompting, taking action rooted in a solid ethical foundation, and overcoming negative thoughts (internally or externally induced). Proactiveness requires freedom from procrastination, continually asking oneself the Golden Question: "What am I waiting for?" and taking the appropriate action to move forward.

Proactiveness means having the courage to do what it takes, without the irrational fear of failure, but being ready for the potential reality of disappointment. It means committing the time and resources to take action that will make a difference.

Being Proactive in the Community

ALTHOUGH THE FOCUS OF THE current book is on proactive action at the individual level, the fact is that we do not operate in this world as single entities. The survival of the human species depends greatly on individuals coalescing together in one way or another to act as one collective unit.

Social cohesion creates synergies that are crucial for the ongoing development and sustenance of the human species. As the English scholar, The Very Reverend John Donne, once wrote in a poem, "No man is an island entire of itself; every man is a piece of the continent, a part of the main...."[65]

Our destinies are intertwined, whether we like it or not. This oneness has become more poignant during the COVID-19 virus pandemic that is ravaging many parts of the world as this book goes to press. The virus was first detected in late 2019 in the Wuhan Province of China. Many people in other parts of the world watched at a distance as China battled the virus day and night in four consecutive months. Little did people realize that in just a few months, COVID-19 would become a global pandemic that would bring almost the entire world to a stand-still.

The virus does not seem to recognize geographical boundaries. Every human being in the world is equally vulnerable.

At the time of writing, hospitals of some western countries are becoming overwhelmed by COVID-19 patients seeking treatment. Many people are also dying. And the trajectory of new infections and deaths does not seem to be slowing down.

The entire world is transfixed by this single and most devastating phenomenon.

It is becoming increasingly clear that everyone in the world is in it together. Many countries are appealing for help from other countries. China, previously demeaned by some media commentators as a pariah communist dictatorship, is currently the country offering the most significant amount of support to other countries in the form of expertise and urgently needed medical supplies.

So, no matter how smart we believe we can become as individuals, we ultimately belong to one or more collective social structures.

The coalescing of individuals into collective units manifests itself in all manner of formal and informal structures. Examples include families, local community groups, professional associations, churches, non-governmental organizations, companies, counties, countries, and regional economic blocks. There are many others. The world thrives on the inter-dependence of the different types of entities. The success of all such collective units depends to a great extent on their proactiveness.

Many entities spend a lot of time defining the collective mission, vision, and goals, with accompanying action plans to achieve the goals. The success of an entity depends on the quality of the plans, but even more importantly, on the ability to execute those plans.

In today's competitive world, it is the entities that plan and execute their plans effectively that tend to achieve great success and grow sustainably over time. Proactiveness is the crucial differentiating factor. And, proactiveness of an entity is a function of the proactiveness of the individuals within the entity.

Some of the best illustrations of the proactiveness of an entity can be found in the business arena. For example, Safaricom PLC started in 1993, has become the largest telecommunications service provider in Kenya. The company had the largest market capitalization on the Nairobi Stock Exchange at the end of February 2020.[66]

In 2018, approximately 49% of the country's GDP was spent through M-Pesa, Safaricom's electronic mobile phone money transfer system. How did Safaricom accomplish this feat, one may wonder? By proactively innovating in a service that solved a significant problem of money transfer between people in Kenya.[67]

So, we all need to be action-oriented to achieve greatness as individuals and as members of different entities.

John Mucai

A Word About Jesus Christ, Prophet Muhammad, and Sri Krishna

JESUS CHRIST, PROPHET MUHAMMAD, AND SRI KRISHNA offered clear guidelines on how everyone needs to live their life to attain the highest level of accomplishment, namely, a spiritual accomplishment that surpasses any other form of human achievement.

No matter how famous or influential an individual may become in this world, they are just a mortal being who will live for a finite period. So, whatever we do to mold ourselves and others to become better individuals, I would suggest that we go one step further. We need to collectively pursue the path to spirituality that we deem most appropriate, to find the true meaning in our lives as individuals and as one united world community.

BIBLIOGRAPHY

"100 Most Influential People in the World" Biography
    Online. Accessed March 12, 2020.
    https://www.biographyonline.net/people/100-most-
    influential.html.Abate, Frank. *The Oxford American Desk
    Dictionary*. New York: Oxford University Press, 1998.

"Beatles by the Numbers." Infoplease. Infoplease. Accessed
    March 20, 2020. https://www.infoplease.com/us/arts-
    entertainment/beatles-numbers.

"Biography John Lennon" Biography Online. Accessed
    March 15, 2020.
    https://www.biographyonline.net/music/john-
    lennon.html.

"Central Messages of Bhagavad Gita." Nitin's Fundas.
    Accessed March 8, 2020.
    http://nseth71.blogspot.com/2014/08/central-
    messages-of-bhagwad-gita.html.

"Financials." Ford Motor Company - Financials. Accessed
    February 16, 2020.

https://shareholder.ford.com/investors/financials/ann
ual-reports/default.aspx.

"Fitzwilliam Notebook." Fitzwilliam Notebook
(Normalized). Accessed March 8, 2020.
http://www.newtonproject.ox.ac.uk/view/texts/norma
lized/ALCH00069#p002.

"Ford Motor Co Market Cap." F Market Cap | Ford Motor
Co - GuruFocus.com. Accessed March 12, 2020.
https://www.gurufocus.com/term/mktcap/F/Market-
Cap-M/Ford-Motor-Co.

"Genghis Khan." Biography.com. A&E Networks TV,
August 30, 2019.
https://www.biography.com/dictator/genghis-khan.

"Genghis Khan - Rise Of Mongol Empire - BBC
Documentary ..." Accessed February 29, 2020.
https://www.youtube.com/watch?v=XAFnxV2GYRU
.

"Genghis Khan Quotes (Author of Genghis Khan's Rules for
(Warriors) Writers)." Goodreads. Goodreads. Accessed
March 23, 2020.
https://www.goodreads.com/author/quotes/5272307.
Genghis_Khan.

"Hemingway's Short Stories." Ernest Hemingway Biography.
Accessed March 10, 2020.

https://www.cliffsnotes.com/literature/h/hemingways
-short-stories/ernest-hemingway-biography.

"Henry Ford Biography." Encyclopedia of World Biography.
Accessed February 16, 2020.
https://www.notablebiographies.com/Fi-Gi/Ford-
Henry.html.

"Historic Kidnapping Cases That Inspire Nightmares."
HistoryCollection.co, October 10, 2019.
https://historycollection.co/historic-kidnapping-cases-
that-inspire-nightmares/12/.

"History - British History in Depth: The Domesday Book."
BBC. BBC. Accessed February 29, 2020.
http://www.bbc.co.uk/history/british/normans/doom
sday_01.shtml.

"Isaac Newton." Biography.com. A&E Networks TV, August
28, 2019. https://www.biography.com/scientist/isaac-
newton.

"Learning to Read" by Malcolm X. Accessed March 14, 2020.
http://accounts.smccd.edu/bellr/readerlearningtoread.
htm.

"Leonhard Euler." Leonhard Euler (1707 - 1783). Accessed
March 9, 2020. http://mathshistory.st-
andrews.ac.uk/Biographies/Euler.html.

"List of Top 100 Famous People" Biography Online.
Accessed February 27, 2020.

https://www.biographyonline.net/people/famous-100.html.

"Martin Luther King's I Have a Dream Speech August 28, 1963." Martin Luther King's I have a dream speech August 28, 1963 < 1951- < Documents < American History From Revolution To Reconstruction and beyond. Accessed February 12, 2020. http://www.let.rug.nl/usa/documents/1951-/martin-luther-kings-i-have-a-dream-speech-august-28-1963.php.

"No Man is an Island" - John Donne. Accessed March 26, 2020. https://web.cs.dal.ca/~johnston/poetry/island.html.

"Philosophy." Wikipedia. Wikimedia Foundation, February 11, 2020. https://simple.wikipedia.org/wiki/Philosophy.

"Religions - Islam: The Qur'an." BBC. BBC, July 14, 2011. https://www.bbc.co.uk/religion/religions/islam/texts/Qur'an_1.shtml.

"Saint Joseph." Biography.com. A&E Networks TV, August 5, 2019. https://www.biography.com/religious-figure/saint-joseph.

"The Autobiography of Malcolm X Quotes by Malcolm X." Goodreads. Goodreads. Accessed March 12, 2020.

https://www.goodreads.com/work/quotes/47400-the-autobiography-of-malcolm-x.

"The Domesday Book." Historic UK. Accessed February 29, 2020. https://www.historic-uk.com/HistoryUK/HistoryofEngland/Domesday-Book/.

"The Nobel Peace Prize 1964." NobelPrize.org. Accessed February 12, 2020. https://www.nobelprize.org/prizes/peace/1964/ceremony-speech/.

"A World of Ideas: The Dictionary of Important Ideas and ..." Accessed March 26, 2020. https://www.amazon.com/World-Ideas-Dictionary-Important-Thinkers/dp/0345437063.

Abdullah, Amatullah. "Prophet Muhammad's Last Sermon: A Final Admonition." The Religion of Islam. Accessed March 7, 2020. https://www.islamreligion.com/articles/523/prophet-muhammad-last-sermon/.

About Famous Artists. Accessed March 12, 2020. http://www.aboutfamousartists.com/index.php/2014/10/michelangelo-and-the-influence-of-lorenzo-de-medici/.

Al Jazeera. "Manhattan DA Reviewing Investigation of Malcolm X Assassination." News | Al Jazeera. Al

Jazeera, February 11, 2020.
https://www.aljazeera.com/news/2020/02/manhattan
-da-reviewing-investigation-malcolm-assassination-
200211164944271.html

Bertram, Christopher. "Jean Jacques Rousseau." Stanford
Encyclopedia of Philosophy. Stanford University, May
26, 2017. https://plato.stanford.edu/entries/rousseau/.

Binlot, Ann. "Discover the African Masks That Inspired
Picasso, Brancusi, Modigliani, and More." Architectural
Digest. Architectural Digest, October 3, 2016.
https://www.architecturaldigest.com/story/foreign-
gods-leopold-museum-vienna.

Buchholz, E. L., Picasso, P., & Zimmermann, B. (2005). *Pablo
Picasso: life and work*. Köln: Könemann, 34.

Buchholz, E. L., Picasso, P., & Zimmermann, B. (2005). *Pablo
Picasso: life and work*. Köln: Könemann, 35.

Castleden, Rodney. *People Who Changed the World*. Eastbourne:
Canary Press, 2011.

CBS News. "The Beatles, by the Numbers." CBS News. CBS
Interactive, February 2, 2014.
https://www.cbsnews.com/news/the-beatles-by-
the-numbers/.

Cellan-Jones, Rory. "Domesday Reloaded Project: The 1086
Version." BBC News. BBC, May 13, 2011.
https://www.bbc.com/news/technology-13395454.

Digital History. Accessed March 12, 2020.
http://www.digitalhistory.uh.edu/disp_textbook.cfm?s
mtid=3&psid=4063.

Dorman, Peter F., and Raymond Oliver Faulkner. "Ramses
II." Encyclopædia Britannica. Encyclopædia Britannica,
inc., July 18, 2019.
https://www.britannica.com/biography/Ramses-II-
king-of-Egypt.

Externe Berichterstattung mittelständischer Unternehmen. Technical
University of Munich, 2010.

Hazlitt, Henry. *Economics in One Lesson: Fiftieth Anniversary
Edition.* Little Rock, AR: Laissez Faire Books, 1996.

HD Pablo Picasso Documentary - YouTube. (n.d.). Retrieved
from
https://www.youtube.com/watch?v=xVEV7CfDngs.

Heck, Alfons. *A Child of Hitler: Germany in the Days When God
Wore a Swastika.* Frederick, CO: Renaissance House,
2001.

Kaku, Michio. "Albert Einstein." Encyclopædia Britannica.
Encyclopædia Britannica, inc., January 14, 2020.
https://www.britannica.com/biography/Albert-
Einstein.

Lipsyte, Robert. "Louisville, Age 12." The New York Times.
The New York Times, March 7, 1971.
https://www.nytimes.com/1971/03/07/archives/-i-

dont-have-to-be-what-you-want-me-to-be-says-
muhammad-ali.html.

Mamiya, Lawrence A. "Malcolm X." Encyclopædia
Britannica. Encyclopædia Britannica, inc., February 17,
2020.
https://www.britannica.com/biography/Malcolm-X.

McGath, T. (2018, September 21). M-PESA: how Kenya
revolutionized mobile payments. Retrieved from
https://mag.n26.com/m-pesa-how-kenya-
revolutionized-mobile-payments-56786bc09ef

Mcneil, Gordon, H. "The Cult of Rousseau and the French
Revolution." *Journal of the History of Ideas* 6, no. 2 (1945):
197. https://doi.org/10.2307/2707363.

Oscar Wilde. AZQuotes.com, Wind and Fly LTD, 2020.
https://www.azquotes.com/quote/1137809 accessed
March 26, 2020.

Scribner, Benjamin M., and Margaret Rose Scribner. *My Life
above the Clouds: in the Footsteps of Henry David Thoreau, as
Lived and Told.* Santa Fe: Sunstone Press, 2015.

Teja, Sai, University of Hyderabad, and University of
Hyderabad. "#1 Most Beautiful Equation in
Mathematics - Euler's Identity." ScienceHook, May 29,
2019. https://sciencehook.com/equations/eulers-
identity-1682.

The Domesday Book Online - Frequently Asked Questions.
    Accessed February 29, 2020.
    http://www.domesdaybook.co.uk/faqs.html#2.
The Editors of Encyclopaedia Britannica. "John Maynard
    Keynes." Encyclopædia Britannica. Encyclopædia
    Britannica, inc., June 20, 2019.
    https://www.britannica.com/biography/John-
    Maynard-Keynes.
The Editors of Encyclopaedia Britannica. "Newton's Laws of
    Motion." Encyclopædia Britannica. Encyclopædia
    Britannica, inc., February 3, 2020.
    https://www.britannica.com/science/Newtons-laws-
    of-motion.
The Life of Mohamed BBC Documentary. Retrieved March
    8, 2020. https://www.youtube.com/watch?v=EBx-
    RYW1FjE&t=4698s
Weatherford, Jack. "Genghis Khan and the Making of the
    Modern World." DiploFoundation. Accessed March 15,
    2020.
    https://www.diplomacy.edu/resources/books/reviews
    /genghis-khan-and-making-modern-world.
Wheen, Francis. *Karl Marx: a Life.* New York: Norton, 2001.
When PABLO became PICASSO Documentary - YouTube,
    (n.d.). Retrieved February 14, 2020, from
    https://www.youtube.com/watch?v=9gjM0BMJrrc

John Mucai

Shakespeare, William. *A Translation, in Greek Iambics, by H. Lushington, from "Julius Cæsar," Act II., Sc. 2.*, 1832. YouTube. YouTube. Accessed February 11, 2020. https://www.youtube.com/watch?v=S64zRnnn4Po.

NOTES

[1] Abate, Frank. *The Oxford American Desk Dictionary*. New York: Oxford University Press, 1998.

[2] "100 Most Influential People in the World" Biography Online. Accessed March 12, 2020. https://www.biographyonline.net/people/100-most-influential.html.Abate, Frank. *The Oxford American Desk Dictionary*. New York: Oxford University Press, 1998.

[3] Al Jazeera. "Manhattan DA Reviewing Investigation of Malcolm X Assassination." News | Al Jazeera. Al Jazeera, February 11, 2020. https://www.aljazeera.com/news/2020/02/manhattan-da-reviewing-investigation-malcolm-assassination-200211164944271.html

[4] Mamiya, Lawrence A. "Malcolm X." Encyclopædia Britannica. Encyclopædia Britannica, inc., February 17, 2020. https://www.britannica.com/biography/Malcolm-X.

[5] "The Autobiography of Malcolm X Quotes by Malcolm X." Goodreads. Goodreads. Accessed March 12, 2020.

https://www.goodreads.com/work/quotes/47400-the-autobiography-of-malcolm-x.

6 "Martin Luther King's I Have a Dream Speech August 28 1963." Martin Luther King's I have a dream speech August 28 1963 < 1951- < Documents < American History From Revolution To Reconstruction and beyond. Accessed February 12, 2020. http://www.let.rug.nl/usa/documents/1951-/martin-luther-kings-i-have-a-dream-speech-august-28-1963.php.

7Digital History. Accessed March 12, 2020. http://www.digitalhistory.uh.edu/disp_textbook.cfm?smtid=3&psid=4063.

8 YouTube. YouTube. Accessed February 11, 2020. https://www.youtube.com/watch?v=S64zRnnn4Po.

9 "The Nobel Peace Prize 1964." NobelPrize.org. Accessed February 12, 2020. https://www.nobelprize.org/prizes/peace/1964/ceremony-speech/.

10 Ibid

11 About Famous Artists. Accessed March 12, 2020. http://www.aboutfamousartists.com/index.php/2014/10/michelangelo-and-the-influence-of-lorenzo-de-medici/.

[12] When PABLO became PICASSO Documentary - YouTube. (n.d.). Retrieved February 14, 2020, from https://www.youtube.com/watch?v=9gjM0BMJrrc

[13] Binlot, Ann. "Discover the African Masks That Inspired Picasso, Brancusi, Modigliani, and More." Architectural Digest. Architectural Digest, October 3, 2016. https://www.architecturaldigest.com/story/foreign-gods-leopold-museum-vienna.

[14] Buchholz, E. L., Picasso, P., & Zimmermann, B. (2005). *Pablo Picasso: life and work*. Köln: Könemann, 34.

[15] HD Pablo Picasso Documentary - YouTube. (n.d.). Retrieved from https://www.youtube.com/watch?v=xVEV7CfDngs.

[16] Buchholz, E. L., Picasso, P., & Zimmermann, B. (2005). *Pablo Picasso: life and work*. Köln: Könemann, 35.

[17] "Henry Ford Biography." Encyclopedia of World Biography. Accessed February 16, 2020. https://www.notablebiographies.com/Fi-Gi/Ford-Henry.html.

[18] "Ford Motor Co Market Cap." F Market Cap | Ford Motor Co - GuruFocus.com. Accessed March 12, 2020. https://www.gurufocus.com/term/mktcap/F/Market-Cap-M/Ford-Motor-Co.

[19] "Financials." Ford Motor Company - Financials. Accessed February 16, 2020.

https://shareholder.ford.com/investors/financials/ann
ual-reports/default.aspx.

[20] Hazlitt, Henry. *Economics in One Lesson: Fiftieth Anniversary Edition*. Little Rock, AR: Laissez Faire Books, 1996.

[21] "List of Top 100 Famous People: ." Biography Online. Accessed February 27, 2020. https://www.biographyonline.net/people/famous-100.html.

[22] Dorman, Peter F., and Raymond Oliver Faulkner. "Ramses II." Encyclopædia Britannica. Encyclopædia Britannica, inc., July 18, 2019. https://www.britannica.com/biography/Ramses-II-king-of-Egypt.

[23] Cellan-Jones, Rory. "Domesday Reloaded Project: The 1086 Version." BBC News. BBC, May 13, 2011. https://www.bbc.com/news/technology-13395454.

[24] "The Domesday Book." Historic UK. Accessed February 29, 2020. https://www.historic-uk.com/HistoryUK/HistoryofEngland/Domesday-Book/.

[25] "History - British History in Depth: The Domesday Book." BBC. BBC. Accessed February 29, 2020. http://www.bbc.co.uk/history/british/normans/doomsday_01.shtml.

26 The Domesday Book Online - Frequently Asked Questions. Accessed February 29, 2020. http://www.domesdaybook.co.uk/faqs.html#2.

27 "Historic Kidnapping Cases That Inspire Nightmares." HistoryCollection.co, October 10, 2019. https://historycollection.co/historic-kidnapping-cases-that-inspire-nightmares/12/.

28 **Castleden, Rodney. *People Who Changed the World.* Eastbourne: Canary Press, 2011.**

29 "Genghis Khan - Rise Of Mongol Empire - BBC Documentary ..." Accessed February 29, 2020. https://www.youtube.com/watch?v=XAFnxV2GYRU .

30 CBS News. "The Beatles, by the Numbers." CBS News. CBS Interactive, February 2, 2014. https://www.cbsnews.com/news/the-beatles-by-the-numbers/.

31 "Beatles by the Numbers." Infoplease. Infoplease. Accessed March 20, 2020. https://www.infoplease.com/us/arts-entertainment/beatles-numbers.

32 "Philosophy." Wikipedia. Wikimedia Foundation, February 11, 2020. https://simple.wikipedia.org/wiki/Philosophy.

[33] Mcneil, Gordon H. "The Cult of Rousseau and the French Revolution." *Journal of the History of Ideas* 6, no. 2 (1945): 197. https://doi.org/10.2307/2707363.

[34] Wheen, Francis. *Karl Marx: a Life*. New York: Norton, 2001.

[35] *Externe Berichterstattung mittelständischer Unternehmen*. Technical University of Munich, 2010.

[36] Ibid, Basu p.68

[37] Ibid, Basu p.69

[38] Heck, Alfons. *A Child of Hitler: Germany in the Days When God Wore a Swastika*. Frederick, CO: Renaissance House, 2001.

[39] "Saint Joseph." Biography.com. A&E Networks TV, August 5, 2019. https://www.biography.com/religious-figure/saint-joseph.

[40] "Religions - Islam: The Qur'an." BBC. BBC, July 14, 2011. https://www.bbc.co.uk/religion/religions/islam/texts/Qur'an_1.shtml.

[41] The Life of Mohamed BBC Documentary. Retrieved March 8, 2020. https://www.youtube.com/watch?v=EBx-RYW1FjE&t=4698s

[42] Abdullah, Amatullah. "Prophet Muhammad's Last Sermon: A Final Admonition." The Religion of Islam. Accessed March 7, 2020.

https://www.islamreligion.com/articles/523/prophet-muhammad-last-sermon/.

[43] "Central Messages of Bhagavad Gita." Nitin's Fundas. Accessed March 8, 2020. http://nseth71.blogspot.com/2014/08/central-messages-of-bhagwad-gita.html.

[44] "Isaac Newton." Biography.com. A&E Networks TV, August 28, 2019. https://www.biography.com/scientist/isaac-newton.

[45] The Editors of Encyclopaedia Britannica. "Newton's Laws of Motion." Encyclopædia Britannica. Encyclopædia Britannica, inc., February 3, 2020. https://www.britannica.com/science/Newtons-laws-of-motion.

[46] "Fitzwilliam Notebook." Fitzwilliam Notebook (Normalized). Accessed March 8, 2020. http://www.newtonproject.ox.ac.uk/view/texts/normalized/ALCH00069#p002.

[47] "Leonhard Euler." Leonhard Euler (1707 - 1783). Accessed March 9, 2020. http://mathshistory.st-andrews.ac.uk/Biographies/Euler.html.

[48] Ibid

[49] Teja, Sai, University of Hyderabad, and University of Hyderabad. "#1 Most Beautiful Equation in Mathematics - Euler's Identity." ScienceHook, May 29,

2019. https://sciencehook.com/equations/eulers-identity-1682.

[50] Scribner, Benjamin M., and Margaret Rose Scribner. *My Life above the Clouds: in the Footsteps of Henry David Thoreau, as Lived and Told.* Santa Fe: Sunstone Press, 2015.

[51] Kaku, Michio. "Albert Einstein." Encyclopædia Britannica. Encyclopædia Britannica, inc., January 14, 2020. https://www.britannica.com/biography/Albert-Einstein.

[52] Lipsyte, Robert. "Louisville, Age 12." The New York Times. The New York Times, March 7, 1971. https://www.nytimes.com/1971/03/07/archives/-i-dont-have-to-be-what-you-want-me-to-be-says-muhammad-ali.html.

[53] Ibid

[54] Ibid

[55]"Hemingway's Short Stories." Ernest Hemingway Biography. Accessed March 10, 2020. https://www.cliffsnotes.com/literature/h/hemingways-short-stories/ernest-hemingway-biography.

[56] "Genghis Khan." Biography.com. A&E Networks TV, August 30, 2019. https://www.biography.com/dictator/genghis-khan.

[57] "Genghis Khan Quotes (Author of Genghis Khan's Rules for (Warriors) Writers)." Goodreads. Goodreads.

Accessed March 23, 2020.
https://www.goodreads.com/author/quotes/5272307.
Genghis_Khan.

58 "Learning to Read" by Malcolm X. Accessed March 14, 2020.
http://accounts.smccd.edu/bellr/readerlearningtoread.htm.

59 Weatherford, Jack. "Genghis Khan and the Making of the Modern World." DiploFoundation. Accessed March 15, 2020.
https://www.diplomacy.edu/resources/books/reviews/genghis-khan-and-making-modern-world.

60 "Biography John Lennon: ." Biography Online. Accessed March 15, 2020.
https://www.biographyonline.net/music/john-lennon.html.

61 Bertram, Christopher. "Jean Jacques Rousseau." Stanford Encyclopedia of Philosophy. Stanford University, May 26, 2017. https://plato.stanford.edu/entries/rousseau/.

62 Oscar Wilde. AZQuotes.com, Wind and Fly LTD, 2020. https://www.azquotes.com/quote/1137809, accessed March 26, 2020.

63 "A World of Ideas: The Dictionary of Important Ideas and ..." Accessed March 26, 2020.
https://www.amazon.com/World-Ideas-Dictionary-Important-Thinkers/dp/0345437063.

---

[64] Shakespeare, William. *A Translation, in Greek Iambics, by H. Lushington, from "Julius Cæsar," Act II., Sc. 2.*, 1832.

[65] 'No Man is an Island' – John Donne. Accessed March 26, 2020.
https://web.cs.dal.ca/~johnston/poetry/island.html.

[66] McGath, T. (2018, September 21). M-PESA: how Kenya revolutionized mobile payments. Retrieved from https://mag.n26.com/m-pesa-how-kenya-revolutionized-mobile-payments-56786bc09ef

[67] Ibid

INDEX

John Mucai

HISTORICAL SNAPSHOTS OF THE GREAT

HISTORICAL SNAPSHOTS OF THE GREAT

Made in the USA
Monee, IL
28 December 2020